The New Plant Collector

The Next Adventure in
Your House Plant Journey

Darryl Cheng

Abrams, New York

Contents

Part I
Caring for Your Collection

1. The New Plant Collector

The last few years have been thrilling for those of us who love plants. Interest in growing house plants exploded. Social media platforms allowed house-plant people to find one another and opened channels where they could enthuse about and promote (and sell and trade) new plant varieties. And growers responded by expanding their offerings with new species and cultivars. It's a whole new world for plant parents.

Today, with some basic skills, you can have an amazing collection of house plants that will bring you great satisfaction over the years. You might have a collection of plants that just came together over time, growing, like a circle of friends, whenever you discovered a new plant that piqued your interest. Or you might be the kind of collector who gets pleasure from finding special varieties of one type of plant. Either way, I'll have ideas and useful advice for you.

As exciting as it is, this new world of house plants is also big and confusing. For this book, I've developed the ABCs of house-plant appreciation to guide you in making choices that will keep you engaged with your plants as they grow and change.

OPPOSITE: Sharing the sunlight with my plant collection.

The ABCs of Houseplant Appreciation

Learn to appreciate your plants in and for themselves, and not just as room décor. The visual richness that plants have to offer is overwhelming. The shape, pattern, texture, or color of a leaf; the growth structure of the overall plant—these are features that bring joy and fascination to the collector. Take leaves, for example. Many familiar plant species have solid-colored leaves, while there are other species or cultivars of the same genus that have variegated leaves. Variegation will introduce a second or third color to a plant's leaves, creating effects that range from striking symmetrical or geometric patterns to random blotches. Collectors get great pleasure from the endless variations. Even a simple "collection" of two plants, where one is a variegated version of the other, will create unexpected aesthetic enjoyment.

BELOW: Here are three variegated varieties of popular plants: *Hoya kerrii variegata*, *Monstera deliciosa* 'Albo Variegata', and Philodendron 'Birkin'.

BIOLOGY

Getting to watch botany unfold is a gift—to witness how another life form goes about its business is fascinating. I got so much pleasure in watching new leaves unfurl on different kinds of plants that I started to make time-lapse videos, just so I could see the details of the whole process in one continuous motion. Plant growth is always rewarding to observe. As Janet Kilburn Phillips says, "There are no gardening mistakes, only experiments." Although it may seem disheartening to have to cut back an overgrown or unbalanced plant, seeing how it propagates and makes new plants is exciting and fulfilling. When you have a collection of plants, some will be beautiful and in peak showing-off form, others may be resting, and still others may be putting out new growth. Once you have more than a few plants, there will always be something interesting happening!

BELOW: Propagation is fulfilling!

A plant can strengthen your connections to people! Maybe it was passed down through generations of your family. Or maybe it was a gift from a good friend. I have many plants that may appear unremarkable, but they hold special meaning to me because they were gifts from friends (one of the greatest rewards of propagating plants is in giving rooted cuttings to other plant collectors). Companionship can also come directly from your plants themselves. Have you cared for a plant long enough that it is uniquely yours? If someone simply replaced it with the identical species, it would not be your special plant. Different plant collections have a way of making different emotional demands. A haworthia collection is like a gang that's easy to get along with, while an anthurium collection can be more like having "difficult" friends who will make you work a bit for their loyalty. Both experiences are important aspects of companionship.

LEFT: Visiting a friend's collection.

So What Makes a Plant Collectible?

Collect what brings you joy! My ABCs of house-plant appreciation—Aesthetics, Biology, and Companionship—invites you to find interest in any plant as you build your collection. Consider the extremely common pothos (epipremnum) varieties with variegated leaves—you probably have a friend who would happily give you a cutting. Each new leaf offers an intriguing surprise (aesthetics). It grows rapidly and is fun to propagate (biology). And you can eagerly share growth updates with your friend (companionship)!

RIGHT: A variegated pothos ready for a trimming can provide many cuttings to share with friends.

Styles of Collecting

As you'll see in this book, there are lots of plants to collect. You'll be happiest if you choose plants that will adapt to your available light conditions and/or your willingness to adapt areas of your living space to creating conditions that different plants need, like adding shelves with grow lights or cabinets that permit you to increase humidity.

Fortunately, a large majority of the plants you're likely to collect cluster in the "bright indirect light" zone (read on and you'll see that I have a strong point of view about what this phrase means). Many are plants in the Arum family, referred to as aroids in the plant community. If you start to read more deeply about house-plant varieties, "aroids" is a word you'll start to see a lot. Aroids grow in the tropics (mostly Central and South America), and the ones that we tend to grow in our homes—aglaonema, alocasia, anthurium, dieffenbachia, epipremnum, monstera, philodendron, rhaphidophora, scindapsus, syngonium, and thaumatophyllum (to name ones you'll find in this book)—are shaded by trees in nature and enjoy filtered sunlight. Like everything else in botany, aroids can become a rabbit hole of information that will swallow you up, so I'll try to strike a balance between giving you a few technical terms to increase your appreciation of these plants and keeping it simple. (That being said, if you are an aspiring aroid collector, a wealth of technical knowledge can be found on the International Aroid Society's website.)

Plants from other genera covered in this book that are fun to collect—like begonia, calathea, ceropegia, ferns, hoya, platycerium, and tillandsia—have similar light requirements to the aroids. However, to get full enjoyment of succulents without grow lights, you'll want more direct sun.

Aside from the practicalities of providing a plant with the conditions it needs to flourish, collecting is about intangibles of taste and interest. It's not unusual to focus on acquiring diverse varieties of a single type of plant, but most people will have several smaller collections. I dedicated a small space on my desk to some interesting succulents. Whenever I need a break from my work, I can simply close my laptop and look at my little haworthia and euphorbia plants, appreciating their unique structures.

If you're just starting, there are some gateway plants that are easy to find and offer fascinating varieties once you get hooked. Of the plants in this book, one starter tillandsia or peperomia will soon lead you to seek out varieties with different characteristics. I covered sansevieria, or snake plants, in my first book, *The New Plant Parent*. Look around plant shops and you'll start to notice an amazing range of leaf forms, from flat swords to thick cylinders.

Beware the Status Symbol Plant

Plant collecting can be an expensive hobby. Let me tell you about tulip mania. In the 1630s, a tulip craze swept Holland, and prices shot up. People were even investing in "tulip futures" for "rare" varieties, as if the flowers were productive assets. The whole market collapsed in 1637, leaving lots of angry people and a big mess for the courts. Of course, when they weren't status symbols anymore, the prices for tulips came back down to earth.

Imagine tulip mania in a world with social media platforms. Influencers entice us with their hot collector plants. Sellers throw the word "rare" in front of any plant to justify charging a premium. This phenomenon is ubiquitous—every consumer category where the product is mostly for personal enjoyment is subject to fabricated demand.

Mike Rimland (VP of R&D, Costa Farms) once made the distinction that there are two ways to look at "rare" when it comes to plants: rare in nature and commercially rare. Rare in nature means the plant species is difficult to find in its natural environment, perhaps because it only grows in a limited range of places, or its habitat is

being reduced by human activity. Collecting these kinds of plants should be done by professional conservationists and it would be unethical to traffic in these plants. You also shouldn't violate laws about importing plants from other countries in your luggage. These laws exist for good reasons.

Commercially rare plants are varieties introduced to the mass market that may not have been widely available before. Such plants are responsibly collected from their natural habitat and put through extensive research to see if they can feasibly be produced on a commercial scale. Or they may be new hybrids created by breeders. These plants are usually expensive when they are novelties (that is, "rare" in the trade), and their price will come down as production increases to meet demand and the eye of fashion moves to newer plants. Of course, there are cases where a certain plant simply does not propagate as readily as others, making it a kind of "small batch" production—these plants will always sell at a premium.

I think you're better off staying away from varieties that are in the middle of a pricing bubble due to hype, but if you must have them, stick to buying or trading cuttings or small plants, and see if you can meet the challenge of growing them successfully. It's discouraging to spend a fortune on a large specimen and then struggle to maintain its perfect appearance in your less-than-perfect growing conditions.

OPPOSITE: Unpacking some plants that are at the expensive end of the spectrum as this book is being written. I hope they make it in my apartment!

Gotta Catch 'Em All!

Living with and Learning from Your Plants

It's always a slippery slope: If one plant can make you this happy, before long every windowsill is occupied, and grow lights become the default light fixtures in your home! Buying lots of plants is easy, but at some point, you may become overwhelmed by the number of plants you're having to move to the shower each week; sometimes, after a few months, the leaf turnover becomes too much of an eyesore, which discourages you from wanting to care for the plant—the cycle of neglect and disinterest continues until you quietly throw away the plant. I've been there! Trust me when I say that you'll be much happier with a few thriving plants than too many "barely surviving" plants. Be realistic about how much time and effort you want dedicate to a plant collection.

If you look at a house plant as décor, then anything that detracts from its perfection will be viewed as "something wrong." The tendency to want to fix things is only exacerbated by the traditional house-plant care advice that changing leaves is a plant's way of saying it's in trouble. Someone probably told you, for example, that yellowing leaves is a sign that you're "overwatering" a plant. Yellowing leaves *might* be a sign that a plant's roots are rotting, but it's just as likely that your plant is responding naturally and healthily to its growing conditions. Most plants let go of older leaves as they grow new ones.

The pricing of some very expensive plants can be based purely on the leaves currently on the plant. Funnily enough, all the grower needs to do is wait for a new leaf, and suddenly the plant can be sold for more. None of those expensive leaves will stay on the plant indefinitely. As new growth continues at the front of the plant, the oldest leaves continually die off. The degree to which the loss of older leaves affects our enjoyment of a plant will vary a lot. Take a *Monstera deliciosa*—if your plant has six very nice leaves and it starts growing a seventh, you're likely to keep enjoying the plant even if you lose the oldest leaf. On the other hand, a plant like *Anthurium warocqueanum* may only have two leaves, and when it starts losing one of them, you'll feel much worse. Even for the same type of plant, the life span of each individual leaf

will vary based on environmental conditions, available nutrients, and so forth. For example, I've documented leaves on my *Monstera deliciosa* that last anywhere from two to four years when planted in a pot (and longer if grown outdoors in its natural habitat).

If your *Monstera deliciosa* is outside and the temperature drops to near freezing, the edges of many leaves (and sometimes the whole leaf) will turn black. These blackened leaf parts will never be green again, so take a moment to mourn their loss and inspect the main vine—if it's still green, there's hope! You can chop up the main vine and start the plant over with new growth from the nodes. Give it a year or two with good growing conditions and you'll have a new plant. When you accept that plants will change, you will take your losses gracefully.

The care guidelines given in this book should be taken as suggestions for long-term enjoyment, not rules to guarantee perfect plants. There are no perfect plants, just as there are no perfect people. If I had to articulate the one way to achieve long-term enjoyment of plants, it would be this: Accept that leaves have a limited life span, aim for growth over decay, and embrace change!

ABOVE LEFT: I'm not going to lose sleep over this yellowing leaf on my *Monstera deliciosa* 'Thai Constellation'.

ABOVE RIGHT: *Anthurium warocqueanum* without nursery conditions will hold on to two or three leaves before one starts retiring (yellowing). I just enjoy each leaf while it lasts.

2. Light: Make It Make Sense

Generations of outdoor gardeners have successfully used this simple classification system for specifying the light that a particular plant requires for growth:

- Full sun: 6 or more hours of direct sun.
- Part sun: 4–6 hours of direct sun.
- Part shade: 4–6 hours of direct sun, preferably NOT hot afternoon sun.
- Shade: less than 4 hours of direct sun.

The system leaves little room for confusion. A garden plant rated for "full sun" would not grow well under the canopy of a large tree, nor would you plant a "shade" plant in the middle of an open field. Gardeners have a good rule of thumb for understanding outdoor light.

When we turn to indoor light and grow lights, things aren't as clear as they should be. We might get a generalized recommendation for a plant based on window direction, as if all windows were the exactly the same size. The catch-all term "bright indirect light," which seems to be what most of our house plants need, is too vague to be useful. Without clear guidelines for giving indoor plants the light they need, we end up believing that some people just have a mysterious gift for growing house plants—hence the myth of the green thumb!

OPPOSITE: Start measuring your indirect light and you'll get clarity on where you should and should not put plants!

ABOVE: For natural light, FC converts to PAR by a factor of roughly 0.2—so if I measure 660 FC using a Lux/FC light meter (left), my PAR meter will read 132 μmol (right).

When I first began collecting plants, I realized that the first step to unraveling the mystery of light for indoor settings, both natural light and grow lights, was to measure it. Your eyes can easily identify when the sun is shining directly on a plant, but the biology of human vision makes it impossible for our eyes to gauge the intensity of indirect light, which is what we call the diffused light that comes from the sky and other surfaces that reflect the sun. Our eyes are constantly rebalancing brightness values as we move through different zones of light, so that we can maintain constancy of vision.

So unless you have superpowers, you'll need a light meter to measure the intensity of indirect light. As with rulers for measuring length, different types of light meters use different scales for measuring light. Your choice will be between one that measures lux (unit: lx) and foot candles (unit: FC), or one that measures PAR photon flux density (unit: µmol).* Both types of meters are adequate to measure natural light and white LED light within the tolerances needed by ornamental plants. Lux/FC meters are considerably less expensive than PAR meters, which makes them the best choice for most people. A lux/FC meter gives you the option to toggle between lux and FC light measurements. For reference, 1 FC equals approximately 10 lux. I use FC, because the FC values for indoor indirect light conditions will be under a thousand. Lux values for the same measurement will be in the thousands and tens of thousands, which makes lux a bit more cumbersome to work with. So be sure to select "FC" when using a Lux/FC meter in conjunction with the recommendations in this book.

For each featured plant genus, I'll give you optimal light conditions for three common lighting scenarios: natural light indoors, grow lights, and commercial nurseries.

*The technical PAR measurement is µmol/m^2/s, which is the number of µmol received in one square meter over a second of time. I've shortened this to µmol.

Natural Light Indoors

Traditional advice about light requirements for plants doesn't account for the two types of indoor light that vary dramatically over the course of a day: direct sunlight (that is, light from the sun that hits a plant directly without bouncing off another object) versus indirect or ambient light (that is, light other than direct sunlight that is bright enough for you to see). Let's rethink our approach to understanding the behavior of light indoors so we can more accurately judge different light situations.

Imagine your plant, sitting near the window all day. If it's a clear day, the sun might shine directly on the plant's leaves for a while, but eventually it will shift out of sight, occluded by the edge of the window. For the rest of the day, the plant will receive light from the ambient brightness of the sky or reflected off of nearby surfaces. Some combination of these two types of light will help the plant grow, and your job is to find the right balance.

Plants Love (Some) Direct Sunlight

Some direct sun is great for the vast majority of plants (and I'll tell you when it isn't). You might have been told that a plant wants "bright indirect light" and will be harmed by direct sun on their leaves. This is a misunderstanding. Sadly, if you put most plants far enough from a window to avoid any direct sun, they're probably not going to get enough light to grow at all. In general, you want to maximize the number of hours your plant is exposed to direct sunlight (indoors, through a window) while avoiding leaf scorch and/or letting the soil reach critical dryness too quickly. The latter point is crucial to understand—the more direct sun your plant receives, the faster it will use up soil moisture, which means you need to stay on top of watering.

OPPOSITE: At this moment, the monstera is receiving direct sun. The plants on the shelf at left are receiving indirect light.

The Intensity of Indirect Light Varies More Than You Think

For the rest of the day, when the sun has moved away from your plant's line of sight, it is now receiving indirect light. The intensity of this light depends on the size of the window and the plant's position relative to the window. To get a feel for the flux of indirect light, use the sensor of your light meter to measure the intensity of the indirect light hitting your plant's leaves several times throughout the day. Meanwhile, watch how the reading changes as you move farther from the window—you'll see that small changes in distance make a big difference. A reading can drop from 400 FC down to 100 FC within an arm's length!

Here are some useful ranges of indirect light to keep in mind:

· Under 100 FC (20 µmol)

· 100–200 FC (20–40 µmol)

· 200–400 FC (40–80 µmol)

· 400–800 FC (80–160 µmol)

Any plant that wants "bright indirect light" will do very well if the indirect light stays in the highest range, 400–800 FC most of the day, and acceptably well at 200–400 FC most of the day.

Too Much Direct Sun? Diffuse It!

If your plant is in the sun and you observe leaf scorching, or you are finding it difficult to keep up with watering it, you can decrease the intensity of the direct sun by using a sheer white curtain to diffuse the sun's rays. When the sun shines directly on a translucent diffusing material, the light will measure anywhere from 800–2,000 FC, which is perfect "bright indirect light." You can also increase the water retention of the plant's substrate (by using less perlite, bark chips, or other draining material). Of course, you can also deal with too much direct sun by moving your plant farther from the window, but you'll also be reducing the intensity of the indirect light that it gets. Use your light meter to be sure you aren't depriving the plant of the light it needs to grow!

The LTH Meter

The light-measuring device shown on the opposite page and throughout the book is the LTH Meter, which stands for "light, temperature, and humidity"—the first device that measures all three. I designed and manufactured it to give plant owners better awareness of the environmental factors needed for optimal growth. The LTH Meter is available on my website, houseplantjournal.com.

TOP LEFT: You can measure light from a plant's point of view by holding your meter next to a leaf.

TOP RIGHT: Without this diffusing material on my window, the *Tillandsia xerographica* would be exposed to direct sun (almost 7,000 FC) for 6 hours, which may make keeping up with watering too challenging. With the diffusing material, my light readings are in the 2,000–3,000 FC range.

BOTTOM RIGHT: Even when the sun is shining directly through a nearby window, the measurement of the indirect light reaching plants out of the path of the direct sunlight can be a modest 200 FC. Luckily, this is fine for an aglaonema.

A Case Study of Indoor Natural Light Levels

LOCATION 1

LOCATION 2

I keep a scindapsus on a bookshelf next to a window. I observe that the sun shines directly on the plant for about one hour. The rest of the day, my spot checks with a light meter show that the indirect light level is in the 200–400 FC range. Let's compare this broad assessment with a more detailed analysis. If you look closely at this photo, you can see two light sensors with blue tips clipped to the bookcase two feet apart: We'll call the one closer to the window **"Location 1,"** and the one farther from the window **"Location 2."**

LOCATION 1

Light Intensity (FC) vs Time

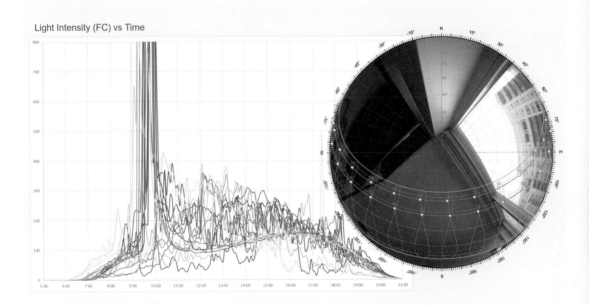

The graph shows light intensity (FC) throughout the daylight hours over two weeks in Toronto, Canada. The sphere is a shade analysis—it shows the plant's-eye view from the shelf. Note that at this location, the plant "sees" a patch of sky as well as a nearby building that bounces light into the window from the sky. The red line is the path of the sun during the period the measurement was taken.

Note the FC spike between the hours of 9:00 and 10:00 am. This is when the sun is in the plant's direct line of sight. After 10:00 am, the sun is elsewhere in the sky and the FC is much lower—the sensor is receiving diffused light (that is, "indirect light") that comes from the sky and reflections off the nearby building. The sensor is registering about one hour of direct sun and in the range of 200–400 FC of indirect light over the rest of the day. This is generally quite good for any "bright indirect light" plant, and it agrees with my estimates based on spot checks.

On the next page, you can see how much the light decreases when we move the sensor just two feet farther into the room.

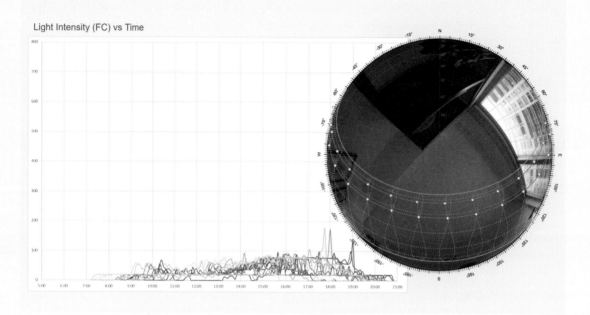

Light Intensity (FC) vs Time

The graph shows light intensity (FC) throughout the daylight hours over two weeks in Toronto, Canada. Note that the shade analysis now shows that the plant is hardly "seeing" any open sky at all.

Over the same two-week period, location 2 receives no direct sun and under 100 FC of indirect sun. The indirect light at location 2 is less than half the indirect light at location 1 because the plant is "seeing" far less area of the surfaces that diffuse the sun's light—in this case, very little of the sky's diffused light is reaching the plant. The strange thing is that your eyes will not register this difference, but a light meter will! With zero direct sun and under 100 FC of indirect light, a "bright indirect light" plant would just survive at location 2. A "low light" plant might be fine.

A RULE-OF-THUMB FOR EVALUATING "BRIGHT INDIRECT LIGHT"

	400–800 FC of indirect light	200–400 FC of indirect light	100–200 FC of indirect light	Under 100 FC of indirect light
4 hours of direct sun	Excellent	Excellent	Excellent	Excellent
3 hours of direct sun				
2 hours of direct sun				
1 hour of direct sun		Good	Good	Fair
No direct sun	Good	Fair	Fair	Poor

A plant growing indoors will see a range of indirect light through most of the day, and, if the sun comes into view, there will be some duration of direct sun. As this chart shows, a longer period of direct sun can compensate for lower levels of indirect light to produce the "bright indirect light" that most house plants need.

Grow Lights

When it comes to grow lights, we need to make a clear distinction between agricultural applications (for example, growing tomatoes exclusively with artificial lighting), where high intensity fixtures are needed, and the maintenance of ornamental plants. This book is only about ornamental plants. White LED lighting is cheap, efficient, and strong enough to grow most of the tropical foliage plants we're likely to collect. So forget about the grow lights you will never need, including fluorescent, ceramic metal halide, high pressure sodium, and pure red/blue LED lights.

In addition to white LED lights, you'll need a light meter to help you position the light at an appropriate distance from the plant to get the desired light intensity. It's also helpful to put your lights on an automatic timer, so you can keep the light on for an appropriate duration every day.

The two key parameters you need to know when using grow lights are the intensity of light at the plant and the amount of time the light is on. I've given recommended settings for the plants featured in this book. Manipulating "total amount of light received" is simple with grow lights, because unlike natural light, the intensity of

the white LED light does not vary over time. For example, let's say your plant is receiving 200 FC x 12 hours and you want to see how an increase of 50 percent will affect its growth. You could increase the intensity by 50 percent to 300 FC and hold the time constant at 12 hours, or you could hold the intensity constant at 200 FC and increase the time by 50 percent to 18 hours. Either way, the plant will be getting 50 percent more light.

Later, we'll introduce the Daily Light Integral concept, which will explain why 300 FC x 12 hours is the same increase as 200 FC x 18 hours.

OPPOSITE: Measure the strength of your white LED grow light at the top of the plant.

Measuring Light in Commercial Nurseries

Here's how the pros do it. From the position of the plant, measure the brightness of the unobstructed sun on a clear day at noon. This will be well over 10,000 FC (about 2,000 μmol). Most of the plants in this book (except the succulents) can tolerate this level of light intensity for a few hours at most. Therefore, commercial nurseries need to block and diffuse direct sun to maximize photosynthesis while minimizing leaf damage via bleaching (they solve the watering problem with automated sprinklers). This is accomplished by using several layers of translucent shade material, which correspond to a specified percentage of shading.

A grower of anthuriums might set their light at 80–90 percent shade, which means the shade material will cut down the sun's rays to roughly 1,000–2,000 FC (200–400 μmol). But a succulent grower might only need 10–20 percent shading, meaning the light should measure in the 8,000–9,000 FC range near midday. In general, every 10 percent of shading reduces the FC reading by 1,000 (assuming no shading is 10,000 FC).

The University of Florida Institute of Food and Agricultural Sciences has published guidelines for commercial growers of many popular house plants, which specify light in terms of percent shading. Even if you don't own a greenhouse, it's important to understand the light levels growers use to efficiently produce high-quality plants. Although your plants can still grow well at a fraction of the light levels of a nursery, it's good to be aware of how far you can push them in terms of light.

OPPOSITE TOP LEFT: A nursery greenhouse diffuses sunlight with overhead translucent material to maintain the optimal light conditions for the plants it's growing.

OPPOSITE TOP RIGHT: A succulent production greenhouse has very thin shading material, so the direct sun is reduced to the 8,000–9,000 FC range.

OPPOSITE BOTTOM: People are often confused because "80–90 percent shading" sounds like a lot of light is blocked, but it's important to remember that we're talking about reduction from completely unobstructed sun (left), not sun through your window (right), where most of the sky is blocked by walls and the ceiling.

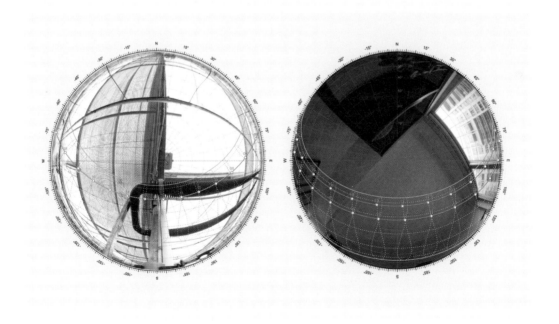

Introducing the Daily Light Integral

The three lighting situations described above—natural light, grow lights, and nursery conditions—are all tied together by a common theme: Different plants have different daily light requirements that must be met for them to thrive. A plant doesn't care if the light it receives comes directly from the sun, or is bounced off a wall, emitted from an LED light, or filtered through a shade. It just needs the right amount of light each day to produce a sufficient amount of carbohydrates. This brings me to the concept of the Daily Light Integral, or DLI. If you're only interested in practical plant care, you can stop reading now and not miss anything, but if you're curious about the bigger picture of house plants and their requirements, you might find that the DLI is a useful concept.

The DLI is the one-stop answer to the question of how much light (in mols) a plant requires in a day. On the facing page, I've listed DLI ranges for the familiar light requirements we attach to plants, ranging from outdoor "full sun" garden plants to "low light" house plants.

In case you were wondering about the power of the sun unimpeded by window glass, let's assume that "full sun" is defined as 6 or more hours of (outdoor) direct sun at 10,000 FC. That's a DLI of 43.2 mol/day.

Lucky for us, most of our house plants will be happy with less than one-quarter of that.

As a reminder, we shouldn't take these numbers as exact prescriptions since ornamental plant growth is a subjective matter—we're not measuring the yield of a vegetable plant. That's why we work with broad overlapping ranges and generalized outcomes.

1–2 mol/day	· Good to maintain "low light" plants · Slow growth for "bright indirect light" plants · Too weak for "shade," "part sun," or "full sun"
2–4 mol/day	· Excellent growth of "low light" plants · Good growth for "bright indirect light" plants · Bare minimum for "shade" · Too weak for "part sun"
4–10 mol/day	· Excellent growth for "low light" plants, keep up with watering/fertilizing · Excellent growth for "bright indirect light" plants, keep up with watering/fertilizing · Good growth for "shade" plants · Low for "part sun" plants
10–20 mol/day	· Very high for "low light" plants, may be difficult to keep up with watering/fertilizing; some leaves may bleach · Very high for "bright indirect light" plants, may be difficult to keep up with watering/fertilizing; some leaves may bleach · Excellent growth for "shade" plants, keep up with watering/fertilizing · Great for "part sun" plants · Too low for "full sun" plants
20–40 mol/day	· Too high for most "low light" and "bright indirect light" plants · Very high for "shade" plants, may be difficult to keep up with watering/fertilizing; some leaves may bleach · Excellent growth for "part sun" plants, keep up with watering/fertilizing · Good growth of "full sun" plants
40+ mol/day	· Too high for "low light," "bright indirect light," and "shade" plants · Very high for "part sun" plants, may be difficult to keep up with watering/fertilizing; some leaves may bleach · Excellent growth for "full sun" plants

MEASURING DLI

It's not practical to try to calculate your DLI in natural light situations, because the light level varies constantly as the motion of the sun across the sky interacts with different daily weather patterns. Assuming you could even collect the hourly light-intensity data at a particular indoor location, you would need a spreadsheet to determine the DLI. You can, however, use DLI to set a grow-light regimen. Because a grow light stays at the same brightness for the length of time it is turned on, calculating DLI calls for simple arithmetic.

Let's say you want to calculate the grow-light requirements for a typical "bright indirect light" plant with a DLI of 6 mol/day, and your plan is to keep the lights on for 12 hours/day. (DLI works with PAR, so if you have an FC meter, you're going to have to take the extra step of converting to FC.)

1. Convert mol/day to μmol/day → 6 x 1,000,000 = 6,000,000
2. Divide by the number of hours lights are turned on in a 24-hour period → 6,000,000 / 12 hours = 500,000
3. Convert μmol/hour to μmol/second → 500,000 / 3,600 = 138.8 μmol/s
4. If you have an FC meter, convert μmol/s to FC → 138.8 / 0.2 = 694.4 FC

So to get to a DLI of 6 mol/day, set up your white LED lights so that the intensity at the top of the plant is around 700 FC or 140 μmol and leave them on for 12 hours/day.

Light Designation	Daily Light Integral (DLI)							
	0	1	2		5		10		15
Full Sun								
Part Sun								
Part Shade								
Shade								
Bright Indirect Light								
Medium Light								
Low Light								

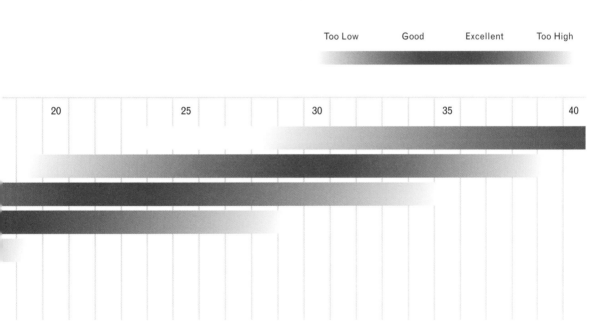

Too Low   Good   Excellent   Too High

20   25   30   35   40

Here's a graphic presentation of
the information on page 35.

3. Soil and Nutrient Management

Let's consider what happens when a plant's roots come into contact with a planting substrate. At the most general level, the substrate holds moisture as a film around each particle. This moisture is available to the roots. Once the particle is holding as much water as it can, any excess will fill up the surrounding pores, or air spaces. If the container has drainage holes, then gravity will pull some of this excess water down through the pot. Over time, the substrate will dry out completely. Some planting substrates hold more water and take longer to dry; others hold less water and dry out more quickly.

Soil Porosity

A typical planting substrate is a combination of water-retaining materials, like potting soil,* and porous materials like perlite that have lower water retention. These porous materials increase the percentage of pore space (porosity) and help prevent soil compaction. The porosity of soil affects how well roots can take up oxygen. If your soil is too dense or compacted (low porosity), root-zone oxygen will be lower and the likelihood of root rot will be higher, thanks to bacteria that thrive in anoxic environments. On the other hand, if soil porosity is too high, you'll find it difficult to keep a plant adequately watered and the roots may not have a firm enough hold on the soil. I've given general recommendations for substrate mixtures for the plants in this book. In almost all cases, you'll want to add some perlite or bark chips to standard potting soil to increase porosity.

* I'm calling this "potting soil" because that's what you'll probably find when you go to the store to buy house-plant potting soil (sometimes it's called, more accurately, "potting mix"). Typically, house-plant potting soil does not contain soil, or dirt! It's likely to be mostly composed of coco coir and/or peat moss with some perlite and/or bark chips.

ABOVE: Larger particles like perlite impart porosity to a planting substrate.

Soil pH

Not only do the soil components have structural characteristics (porosity), but they can also have different pH values, from acidic to basic. Plants evolve in different pH environments, and the wrong soil pH for a particular plant may cause nutrients it needs to become unavailable. There's no single pH value that will work for every plant, but if I had to generalize for the majority of the plants listed in this book, it would be neutral to slightly acidic. Measuring pH is something that commercial nurseries do on a regular basis, but as a hobbyist I've never really found the need to do this. If you just repot your plant from time to time and make sure you are flushing your soil often, your pH will stay within what is expected of your planting substrate.

BOTTOM LEFT: Older spider plant leaves inevitably develop some tip browning. Not a big deal.

BOTTOM RIGHT: About a month ago, I took cuttings from this *Monstera deliciosa*, leaving just one leaf on this vine. That single leaf took on the mineral accumulation that would have normally been shared by multiple leaves, resulting in rapid tip browning. Not to worry—new growth will appear in a few weeks so you can let this leaf retire.

Mineral Accumulation

Whenever you water your plant (unless it's with distilled water), trace minerals will be transferred to the soil. Over repeated wetting and drying cycles, these minerals can accumulate in the soil. Mineral salts from fertilizers also build up gradually. High concentrations of some minerals can be detrimental to a plant. Regular soil flushing mitigates the negative impact of mineral accumulation (see the flushing technique explained in the watering section). Over the longer term, repotting plants effectively resets most mineral accumulation problems.

Beware of plant perfectionism. You may be tempted to use distilled water and spend a lot of time (and water) flushing your soil, hoping to completely mitigate any leaf blemishes—don't fall for this trap! Remember that leaves have a limited life span and your long-term goal is to encourage NEW growth. If you make plant care all about maintaining leaf perfection, you will constantly be disappointed! Use the cleanest water you have available, occasionally flush your soil, and thank each leaf when it inevitably retires. When your light is good and you're watering/fertilizing accordingly, new leaves will outnumber older ones dying off.

Fundamental Nutrients for Plant Health

The fourteen essential plant nutrients can be broadly categorized into macronutrients (nutrients required in large quantities) and micronutrients (nutrients required in small quantities). This is good information to have, so here they are:

Macronutrients
Nitrogen, Phosphorus, Potassium, Calcium, Sulfur, Magnesium.

Micronutrients
Iron, Boron, Chlorine, Manganese, Zinc, Copper, Molybdenum, Nickel.

These nutrients are important because your plants need them to construct their cells and maintain their functions. In nature, the activities of animals, insects, fungi, and microbes make some of these nutrients available to plants. In fact, research has shown that plants exude sugary substances to attract specific fungi and bacteria that, in exchange, provide the plant with nutrients. A house plant is cut off from these biological contributors to its needs, which is why you need to add fertilizer.

One reason plants look so "perfect" when grown in a greenhouse is that nutrients and light are calibrated precisely to their needs, whereas plants in nature reflect the varying conditions in which they were raised. These plants have a different type of beauty. Plants in the jungle don't look "out of place"; the shape they've taken communicates "we belong here!"

3-1-2 Fertilizer

Luckily, you don't need to worry about fourteen nutrients when you fertilize your plants. Almost all fertilizers are characterized by an NPK ratio, which describes the percentage by volume of nitrogen, phosphorous, and potassium, the top three macronutrients (I would avoid buying a fertilizer without an NPK ratio). Other nutrients will be listed if they're present, but for everyday house-plant enjoyment, you won't bother about them.

While you could try to learn the optimal NPK ratio for every plant, here's why the ratio 3-1-2 is all you really need. Consider the type of plant you're growing: The focus of this book is growing foliage plants. We are most interested in the leaves. Nitrogen is a key component in chlorophyll, which is most concentrated in the leaves. Any high-nitrogen fertilizer will benefit our foliage plants. More specifically, regarding the ratio 3-1-2, every resource for commercial foliage-plant production suggests using this ratio for virtually all house plants.

Any multiple of 3-1-2 (or close to it) will work just fine. You may encounter any of the following: 24-8-16, 9-3-6, 12-4-9, 11-3-8, and slight variations thereof. Note that the higher numbers do not mean that the fertilizer is stronger. It just means the formula is more concentrated—you should follow the mixing directions listed on the packaging.

Most fertilizers are sold as powders, crystals, or liquid that you stir into your watering can, following directions regarding the amount to add per quart or gallon. Then, when you water your plant, you're also delivering nutrients. I fertilize my plants each time I water with a highly concentrated liquid fertilizer. I use a pipette to add the fertilizer to the watering can and then fill it with water. No further mixing required.

Lately, I've been experimenting with slow-release formats that you put directly into the soil. I use fertilizer pellets that can be mixed into soil and worm castings, also mixed into soil, usually during repotting. The idea is that each time you water, a little bit of the fertilizer gets leached off the pellet and feeds your plant. So far, I'm pleased with the results.

TOP LEFT AND RIGHT: Liquid fertilizer needs to be diluted into your watering can. Make sure you follow the mixing instructions.

BOTTOM: Slow-release fertilizer—the little yellowish pellets get mixed into the substrate and release a small amount of fertilizer every time they get watered.

4. Watering: A Universal Approach

We're all used to getting specific instructions about how often to water different types of plants. When I looked at commercial foliage production guidelines, however, I found that they gave specific suggestions for light levels and fertilizer quantity, but no mention of how frequently to water. That's because when light levels, soil structure, and nutrients are within acceptable parameters, watering is based on observed soil dryness, not a specific frequency based on plant type. With this approach, there's no need to keep track of when you watered—you simply look at and feel the soil to determine its dryness level and decide whether or not to water. You may develop a watering schedule, but it will be based on the soil reaching the appropriate level of dryness with a predictable frequency.

OPPOSITE: Observation of soil dryness is the key to knowing when to water.

We seem to like the notion that "every plant has different needs." This is the path to confusion. We start with a plant type and prescribe a watering frequency, then we start listing exceptions:

"How often should I water a snake plant?"

"About every two or three weeks, but if it's getting lots of light, it could be every week; but in the winter, it will be less frequent."

The problem lies in our desire for a specific watering schedule for a specific plant. The question should really be, "At what soil dryness level should I water a snake plant?" This is somewhat awkward to say, but it's exactly how you should THINK about watering.

Let's put this idea to the test: "Water a snake plant whenever its soil is completely dry." If the plant sits in front of a huge bay window receiving several hours of direct sun, the soil will be completely dry in a few days. If it's positioned at a distance from your window, the soil could take a few weeks to become completely dry. It is often stated that one should water less in the winter because there is less light, but winter air is also drier, resulting in faster transpiration and water usage. If you simply observe the soil and wait for "completely dry" as your cue to water, you don't need to factor environmental conditions into some complex calculation. Just assess the soil and decide whether to water.

For each plant in this book, I'll give watering instructions in relation to soil dryness.

You only need to distinguish between a few levels of soil moisture to use as your cue to water. You can probe with your fingers or a chopstick. In time, you can learn to gauge the extra weight of the water by lifting the pot. A moisture meter, which typically shows 8–10 levels between wet and dry, is not necessary.

Every plant will fall into one of these three categories:

ABOVE: Maidenhair fern (left) and some calatheas (right) enjoy consistently moist soil.

"Keep Evenly Moist"

In this watering strategy, it's time to water when the soil is slightly drier than fully saturated. For a small plastic nursery pot, you can easily lift the plant every few days to check the difference in weight.

"Water When Partially Dry"

The cue to water this kind of plant is when the soil is somewhat dry, say in the 50–70 percent dry range. The majority of potted tropical foliage plants will welcome this watering strategy.

"Water When Completely Dry"

In this watering strategy, you will not water the plant until its soil is completely dry. Most cacti and succulents fall into this watering category. When the soil has reached this dryness, you will completely and thoroughly saturate it—don't just pour a few drops!

How to Water

Quick pour

If you have lots of plants and little time, you can pour a small amount into each one to bring the soil to the point of being "lightly moistened." I wouldn't do this all the time, as the uneven moistening of soil will leave dry pockets where roots, and the corresponding leaves, may die off.

Bottom watering

This is when you sit a pot, typically a plastic nursery pot with drainage holes, in a bowl of water, allowing it to soak into the potting medium through the drainage holes. Depending on your soil properties, the depth of the pool of water, and the duration of soaking, the soil will generally reach a moistened state somewhere between lightly moist and fully saturated. Bottom watering is gentle, but it doesn't promote as much oxygen exchange or mineral leeching as top watering.

Thorough watering

This is when you water the planting medium thoroughly to the point where any additional water you pour in is immediately coming through the drainage hole. Then the soil is considered "fully saturated." This way of watering is most effective when done in a sink or shower, but if you're careful, you can do it anywhere. It's helpful to have a kitchen baster for when the saucer under the pot starts to overflow!

OPPOSITE TOP: Quick pour (left) and bottom watering (right)

OPPOSITE BOTTOM: A sink or shower is useful for thorough watering and soil flushing.

Soil flushing

Think of this as a super-thorough watering. After repeated watering cycles, your plant's soil may begin to accumulate mineral salts from fertilizers, or even from the water itself. Flushing leeches these minerals out of the soil. Ideally, you'd do this in a sink or shower: Providing that your plant is in a container with drainage holes and your faucet is high enough, you can just run a gentle stream of water into the soil for a while. You can also do it by pouring. I don't flush at every watering, maybe once a month. While you may be tempted to flush all the time in an attempt to prevent leaf tips from browning, don't waste your time (and water)! Remember that leaves have a limited life span, which includes eventually bearing the marks of transpiration and the collateral damage of mineral accumulation. Flushing washes away water-soluble nutrients, so I finish by watering with fertilized water.

Overwatering: A Terrible Concept

If you worry about "overwatering" a plant, then you probably think that if you water it less, it will thrive. But if your soil is never drying out and the plant's roots are rotting, watering less won't solve the plant's problem. Root rot is usually caused by a plant not getting enough light and growing in soil that's too compacted. A plant that's just sitting in a dark corner and not photosynthesizing will inevitably disappoint you no matter how carefully you water it.

Use Tap Water

As you grow a wider variety of plants, you'll start to hear warnings about how chlorine in tap water will harm them. Common advice is to let your water sit overnight to allow the chlorine to dissipate. I would hate for you to delay watering a thirsty fern because you forgot to fill up your watering can the night before!

It's true that chlorine buildup can be associated with browning leaves, and some plants are more sensitive to this than others. And the amount of chlorine in tap water does vary from place to place. I just don't think you should waste your energy worrying about things that are out of your control, and the chemicals in your tap water are definitely out of your control. Focus your energy on optimizing light and fertilizing and try using your tap water for a while. You may find that you can accept the rate of leaf turnover.

My own philosophy of using tap water is aligned with the principle of natural selection, namely that whatever water comes from my tap is what my plants get and whichever plants grow well get to stay. Those that are negatively affected to the degree that they are no longer presentable will be rejected. I don't have to own every possible plant, and neither do you.

Of course, you're welcome to use distilled or RO water. The leaves of some of your plants will stay nicer looking for longer than if you were to use heavily chlorinated tap water. However, all plants have a natural cycle of growth and decay regardless of what water you use.

OPPOSITE: All of these snake plants get the "water when the soil is completely dry" strategy.

5. Home Setups

The trick with collecting plants at home is finding the right balance between what works for you and your living space and the plants' needs and their growing space. If you live in a smaller apartment with other people, you may need to limit the number of plants you own to keep the space aesthetically pleasing. If you like sitting by the window soaking up the sun, you may have to share that space with your plants. If you have space but not a lot of natural light, you'll need to learn how to use grow lights.

If you want to create optimal environmental conditions for plants that need high humidity, you could set up a greenhouse cabinet. If you have extra storage space, you could have a dedicated grow tent, but you'll be visiting your plants rather than living with them. With outdoor space, a hobby greenhouse could house your entire collection.

You can start by collecting plants that will thrive in your available natural light. Consider a light meter and use my chapter on light to do a natural-light assessment. Once you have a good understanding of the duration of direct sun and the range of indirect light from your windows, you can focus on the kinds of plants that will do well and how close to the windows they'll need to be to thrive without added grow lights.

OPPOSITE: A cabinet full of collectible anthuriums.

Plant Shelving

If you want to maximize your plants' access to natural light and are dealing with relatively small plants (6-inch pots or smaller), you can put them on a shelf that raises them just up to the level of the windowsill. Sturdy glass shelves allow light to reach the lower levels, and they don't block too much of your view of the outside.

OPPOSITE: A cabinet with open shelving is called an étagère. One with adjustable shelves can create visual interest and accommodate different plant heights.

ABOVE: This plant shelf replaced my blinds.

RIGHT: Ladder shelves lit by a skylight.

Grow Lights

White LED technology has made growing plants under artificial lights relatively simple and affordable. Options range from cheap, flexible lights that are thin and light-weight enough so that they can be mounted anywhere to more substantial fixtures fitted with long T5 and T8 lights that can provide even light to a wider surface. Small-succulent enthusiasts appreciate the latter type of setup because it allows them to arrange many plants in a small area. Even a windowless corner can be lit with a grow light: A collection of tropical foliage plants can be adequately lit (around 200 FC for 12 hours a day) by a single grow light if it's powerful enough. Because of the enormous number of product choices for different situations, you'll want to do research based on your specific needs. You could start with my posts about grow lights on houseplant-journal.com.

LEFT: LED lights are lightweight and release minimal heat, which makes them very easy to install on shelves. There's no skylight at my mother's new home, so I helped her install white T5 LED grow lights under each shelf.

RIGHT: Cheaper clamp lights can be brought in to supplement light in the winter months. Their lower output is suitable for a small plant at close range. The plant in this setup is seeing about 800 FC (160 μmol).

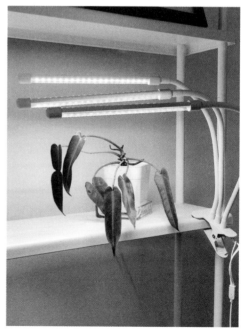

Greenhouse Cabinet

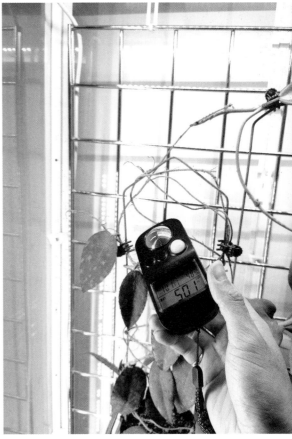

At the next level of environmental control, a popular way to grow humidity-loving aroids is by creating an Ikea greenhouse cabinet. White LED grow lights can be easily mounted anywhere in the cabinet, and small fans can provide vital air flow. (In truth, any glass cabinet can be an "Ikea greenhouse cabinet"; the only advantage to using an Ikea cabinet is that there are lots of online resources to show you hacks with specific Ikea models to get them set up for growing plants.)

ABOVE: The only way to know if your plants are getting enough light (or too much) is by measuring it. These hoyas will be very happy with 500 FC for 12 hours a day.

ABOVE LEFT: Three T8 LEDs mounted in a greenhouse cabinet.

ABOVE RIGHT: With good weather stripping to seal up the gaps, high humidity can be easily maintained even without a humidifier, as long as the potting substrates are moist.

RIGHT: A glass display cabinet converted into a mini greenhouse creates a wonderful display and a nicely controlled environment thanks to LED lights and mini fan.

Grow Tent

If you are fortunate to have a lot of extra space (basements are good for this), you can consider setting up a grow tent. The walls are typically lined with mylar, which is a highly reflective surface meant to minimize light loss. You'll need white LED lights and a fan to keep air circulating. A humidifier can be useful as well. Tents come in many sizes, with or without LED lights and fans included. You'll want to plan carefully and research your options.

LEFT: Tim's grow tent setup is nearly packed to the brim with three-tiered shelving.

RIGHT: Brian's unfinished basement allowed him to use a large portion for a grow tent filled with rare aroids. A bit of water splashing is not a big concern on unfinished concrete floors.

Hobby Greenhouse (Outdoor)

This is the ultimate home-based grow space, like having a little slice of a commercial greenhouse. Of course, unless you live in the tropics or you heat your greenhouse, you won't be using it year-round. Depending on the plants you are collecting, you will need to consider how much to filter the sun. Most home-based greenhouses use a plastic panel that diffuses the sun's light. If you are growing mostly succulents and cacti, the diffusion panel alone will work well. Aroids and other lower-light plants would benefit from an added shade cloth.

ABOVE: Alison's greenhouse faces south with few obstructions, so a shade cloth is used on the roof during the summer to keep light levels in check. It's an aroid paradise!

Part II
Plants to Collect

Aglaonema

Aglaonema has been a "typical" house plant for many decades. Take a look through an old home-décor magazine and you might find an Aglaonema 'Silver Bay' brightening a dark corner, where it could never thrive in real life. While aglaonema is often touted as doing great in "low light," you won't see much growth unless the ambient light levels are above 100 FC (20 μmol) for most of the day. That's not as far from a window as you might think!

The different varieties of aglaonema you'll find at plant shops all feature interesting leaf patterns. Many are hybrids bred by growers from more than one species. *Aglaonema nitidum, A. commutatum, A. costatum*, and *A. rotundumare* are commonly used for breeding new hybrids.

By the way, hybrids that have commercial value are given trade names, which take the form Genus 'Hybrid Name'. A plant bred from one species is called a cultivar and takes the form, Species 'Cultivar Name'. So, for example, among the aglaonemas illustrated in this section, Aglaonema 'Anyamanee' is a hybrid, while *Aglaonema pictum* 'Tricolor' is a cultivar. (A plant species' scientific name is always made up of its genus and its species: that way, you know that *Aglaonema pictum* is a species in the genus *Aglaonema*. In lists of plants in the same genus, the genus name will often be abbreviated to its first letter to save space, as in *A. pictum* 'Tricolor'.)

OPPOSITE: Some aglaonema hybrids feature brilliant pink splashes, like Aglaonema 'Anyamanee' (right).

ENVIRONMENT

Natural light: You should get adequate growth if your average indirect light is above 100 FC (20 µmol), but the plant will do much better in the 400–800 FC range (80–160 µmol). With adequate watering, Aglaonema can tolerate 1–2 hours of direct sun. Use a white sheer curtain to diffuse the sun if the duration of direct exposure will be longer.

Grow light: If you're using a modest grow light setup, place an aglaonema so that it will receive at least 200 FC (40 µmol) for 12 hours/day, equivalent to DLI 1.7 mol/day, for good growth.

Nursery light: Aglaonema are produced with 90 percent shade, which translates to around 1,000 FC most of the day.

Temperature and Humidity: Aglaonema will grow well with daily temperatures in the 21–29 C (70–85 F) range. Most will grow well with average room humidity (40–60 percent), but some prefer a little higher (60–80 percent) to maintain very nice leaves.

EFFORT

Watering: Although aglaonema are drought tolerant, they will do best if watered when partially dry. As the soil reaches total dryness leaves will droop, although the main stem should remain upright on a larger plant. The plant will perform better if you avoid letting the soil dry out completely between waterings.

Fertilizing: A fertilizer with NPK ratio 3-1-2 will be suitable.

Substrate: Standard potting soil (2 to 3 parts) with some added perlite or bark chips (1 part). Use more drainage material if light levels are expected to be on the lower side.

EXPECTATIONS

With good light and fertilizing, the top of the plant should keep a nice set of leaves, although growth patterns vary a bit across different cultivars of aglaonema. *Aglaonema pictum* 'Tricolor', with camouflage-patterned leaves, tends to hold on to very few leaves as it grows, making the plant look rather sparse as it gets taller. When you want a more compact plant, you can air layer the top portion or simply cut it off and get it to root in water or sphagnum moss. Stem sections can be cut into pieces and laid into sphagnum moss sealed in a container. New growth points will emerge to form new plants. Some aglaonemas readily put up pups, which can be separated and potted up on their own or left with the mother plant to create a fuller look.

Aglaonema Varieties to Collect

TOP LEFT: *Aglaonema rotundum* is a little less widely available.

ABOVE RIGHT: Top left: *Aglaonema* 'Silver Bay', bottom left: A. 'Spring Snow', right: A. 'Maria'.

BOTTOM LEFT: *Aglaonema pictum* 'Tricolor' is a highly desirable plant to collect.

Two Years with Aglaonema 'Jubilee'

The window space was full, so I installed this metal grid, typically used for retail displays, as a plant shelf. From this position, the plant got around 400 FC (80 μmol) for 12 hours/day—growth was quite good. I used a 3-1-2 fertilizer at every watering.

A friend bought a large aglaonema (not 'Jubilee') that happened to have this A. 'Jubilee' pup hiding in its pot. I removed the pup to start my own journey!

3 months

It seems we have hit the balance point of leaf turnover: This round of new leaves came with shedding of the lower few leaves. A repotting will hopefully allow the plant to hold on to more leaves at a time.

Within the year, this plant has produced two pups. I keep them in the pot to give the plant a fuller look.

From the front, the two pups below the original plant help to cover up the bare lower stem.

1 year, 8 months

2 years

1 year

During this time, my wife and I moved to a new apartment with some nice large windows. This plant got a premium spot: Front row seats in an east-facing window where it got about 2 hours of direct sun and indirect light in the 400–600 FC range (~80–120 µmol).

A flower—my plant is going through botanical puberty! Some cultivation guides recommend cutting off the flowers to allow the plant to focus energy on the leaves, but I find it fascinating to watch the flowers grow and fade.

This is the oldest stem after about two years. It bears the marks of leaves past, but the stem has all the necessary tissue to produce new roots—so if I decide that this one shoot is too tall, I can take a cutting, get it to root, and plant it into the pot. A new shoot can also grow out from the severed stump, making for a lusher plant when it matures.

Alocasia

When I first began my plant journey, I encountered a lot of bad press around alocasias. Yes, their foliage is highly attractive, but they also seemed to have the perfect storm of attributes that make a plant type "difficult" to own, especially the high probability of leaf turnover in most indoor spaces. Your gateway alocasia will likely be the Alocasia 'Amazonica', which has dark glossy leaves with contrasting midribs.

Even the undersides of the leaves are interesting, with fine veining reminiscent of a suburban road map. The shape of the leaves makes the gamer in me think about leveling up an alien-looking shield. The challenge: The ideal environmental conditions for alocasia are rare to find in a typical indoor space—namely the plant's demanding light and temperature requirements! And the plant's life cycle (in certain conditions) can be shocking to a new collector experiencing total dieback with not a single leaf left. Read on to get a better understanding of the environmental conditions needed for good growth and what to expect from the plant's life cycle—for less panicking!

OPPOSITE: One of the most common alocasias available for sale is a hybrid of *A. sanderiana* and *A. watsoniana*. The resulting plant was given the name Alocasia 'Amazonica', after the nursery where it originated, Amazon Nursery in Miami, Florida.

ENVIRONMENT

Natural light: Ensure the indirect light is 200–400 FC (µmol) most of the day. If you can also get 2–3 hours of direct sun, that would be great.

Grow light: Set the light at a height such that the plant receives 1,000 FC (200 µmol) for 12 hours—this is a DLI of 8.6 mol/day.

Nursery light: Alocasia are sometimes used for landscape planting with the designation Part Sun/ Part Shade, which suggests their preferred DLI range is anywhere from 10 mol/ day up to 30 mol/day. In a nursery, a 50 percent shade cloth would diffuse the sun to around 5,000 FC for most of the day.

Temperature and Humidity: Alocasia will grow well in warmer temperatures (22–29 C or 72–85 F) and average room humidity (40–60 percent). You will notice earlier dieback in slightly cooler temperatures, which, in its natural environment, signals the onset of winter.

EFFORT

Watering: While there are active leaves, it is best to keep the plant evenly moist in good light. With lower light levels, you can stretch the watering a bit to water when about halfway dry, but don't expect amazing growth.

Fertilizing: A fertilizer with NPK ratio 3-1-2—either liquid or slow-release will work.

Substrate: Standard potting soil (3 to 4 parts) with some added perlite or bark chips (1 part). Use more drainage material if light levels are expected to be on the lower side.

EXPECTATIONS

Alocasia are sold with up to three stems with mature leaves—the juvenile leaves may have already retired by this point. With good light, a few more leaves should grow before you start seeing the older leaves dying off. If your temperatures tend to be on the cooler side of the range (say 19–22 C or 66–72 F), expect to see most, if not all, of your leaves die off one by one. If this occurs, there is no need to panic— simply repot the base of the plant into new soil and try to keep it warmer, around 25–29 C or 77–85 F if possible, and make sure the substrate is evenly moist. This may trigger new growth. Corms can also be separated and planted into moist sphagnum moss and kept at high humidity to encourage germination. (A corm is a small bulb attached to the plant's root system.) You will have several new plants that will start off small but should progressively get larger leaves as new ones emerge.

LEFT: Removing a corm from the base of my unpotted alocasia.

Alocasia Varieties to Collect

ABOVE LEFT: *Alocasia macrorrhiza* 'Stingray'—as the name suggests, the leaf shape develops features like wings and a tail.

ABOVE RIGHT: An emerging Stingray leaf is a thrilling sight!

RIGHT: *Alocasia baginda* 'Dragon Scale'.

ABOVE: *Alocasia cuprea*: the coppery red texture almost looks like an alien armor.

LEFT: *Alocasia micholitziana* 'Frydek': A similar shield shape to the A. Amazonica, but with a deep-green velvet texture. May also be found with variegation (and may also be a lot more expensive!).

OPPOSITE: *Alocasia zebrina*: one of the few examples where the main feature of the plant is the stem. This older leaf is ready to retire.

Aloe

When people hear "aloe," they mostly think about aloe vera and how it is good to put on burns. The Aloe genus has many other species and hybrids that are lots of fun to grow and collect—although they're not the greatest for your skin. Their thick, fleshy leaves store lots of moisture so they are well-adapted to long periods of dryness. With adequate light and just the right amount of water stress (that is, you withhold water), many aloes will get a reddish to purple tint.

OPPOSITE: A collection of aloe growing up and nearly ready for sale.

The New Plant Collector

ENVIRONMENT

Natural light: Aloe will grow very well if it can get 3–4 hours of direct sun while, at other times of the day, the indirect light should be as high as possible, in the 400–800 FC (80–160 µmol) range.

Grow light: Set your aloe to receive at least 800 FC (160 µmol) for 12 hours—this will be a DLI of 6.9 mol/day. Going higher is fine—for example 1,000 FC (200 µmol) for 16 hours makes the DLI 11.5 mol/day.

Nursery light: Aloe are produced with Full Sun to Part Shade. In a controlled commercial setting, only light shading (10–20 percent) is used, which is 8,000–9,000 FC (1,600–1,800 µmol) for most of the day.

Temperature and Humidity: Aloe will grow well with daily temperatures in the 13–35 C (55–95 F) range. Dry to average room humidity is fine (20–60 percent).

EFFORT

Watering: Aloe should only be watered once its substrate is completely dry. You can even wait until the leaves are just slightly less firm before watering.

Fertilizing: Aloe are not heavy feeders so you can use a diluted 3-1-2 fertilizer every other watering.

Substrate: The ideal aloe substrate will be fast draining but dense enough to support the weight of the plant. One part coir (or peat moss) with one part coarse sand is suitable.

EXPECTATIONS

Aloe are relatively slow growers, but after a few years there should be some pups forming at the base of the plant. These can be removed and transplanted to new pots. The main plant can be supported with stakes, but you may eventually want to cut and propagate the top as the lower leaves die off, leaving behind a bare stem. Some aloe do not need to be separated for several years, forming a nice clump of plants.

Aloe Varieties to Collect

ABOVE LEFT: Aloe 'Delta Lights' grows in a neat rosette with textured green and white leaves.

ABOVE RIGHT: *Aloe aristata* forms a tight, compact shape with glossy leaves.

RIGHT: Two unknown aloes produced seeds that Jeff Mason, from Mason House Gardens, grew into this cluster of plants after several years—he calls it the Unnamed Jeff Mason Hybrid (left). I was given a pup from that plant (right) and I'm excited to grow my own little colony!

Aloe 'Christmas Carol'—a
hybrid aloe NOID (for "no ID,"
used to describe a plant of unknown parentage). NOIDs can
occur when many plants of the
same genus are growing close
together and cross-pollinate.

Observations of Two Aloes

Day 1

A sun-stressed Aloe x nobilis and two recently separated pups. Be cautious when handling this variety of aloe—it has sharp teeth!

A few weeks later

With a good soaking, the plant will regain its bright green color in a few weeks.

4 years later

The Aloe x nobilis (left) has graduated into a larger pot. I decided to keep this set of pups together in the same pot. *Aloe arborescens* (right) has put on lots of growth after a summer outdoors, mostly shaded by a tree.

Here's the *Aloe arborescens* 7 years earlier, when I first got the plant.

Anthurium

Perhaps you've seen the very common red-flowered anthurium (*Anthurium andraeanum*) at your local grocery store. This has long been a house-plant staple, with a range of flower colors available if you look for them. More ambitious collectors soon seek out anthuriums with exotic foliage— dark, velvety-textured leaves with striking vein patterns in many shapes and sizes. For the highly motivated grower, growing and even hybridizing anthuriums from seed is a rewarding experience.

OPPOSITE: Several young velvety anthuriums to start off my collection: Left to right, front row, *Anthurium clarinervium, A. regale, A. crystallinum*; back, *A. magnificum.*

ENVIRONMENT

Natural light: Ensure the indirect light is in the 200–400 FC (40–80 µmol) range. If the duration of direct sun exceeds 1–2 hours, then block it with a white sheer curtain.

Grow light: Anthuriums grow under a forest canopy where the DLI can be anywhere from 2 to 10 mol/day, depending on how dense the canopy is. Achieving this is possible with cheaper grow lights—ensure the measurement at the leaf is at least 200 FC (40 µmol) and keep the light on for 12 hours/day.

Nursery light: Commercially grown Anthurium enjoy 80–90 percent shade, which will measure 1,000–2,000 FC (200–400 µmol) and lasts most of the day. An equivalent grow light, measuring 1,000 FC (200 µmol) on for 12 hours/day would give a DLI of 8.6 mol/day. If you are giving your anthurium this level of light, make sure you are keeping up with watering and fertilizing.

Temperature and Humidity: Anthuriums will grow best in the temperature range of 15–32 C (60–90 F) and humidity 60–80 percent. At lower humidity (30–50 percent) certain types of anthurium may experience minor leaf deformities and leaves may have difficulty emerging from their sheath. Misting the emergent leaf can help with this.

EFFORT

Watering: Water an anthurium when its substrate reaches about halfway dry. If your light levels are on the higher side, you could increase your watering frequency, cycling between just slightly dry and saturated. Anthuriums will recover from drought, but their growth may be stunted.

Fertilizing: Support those big leaves with a good 3-1-2 fertilizer or a slow-release fertilizer added to the substrate.

Substrate: Standard potting soil or sphagnum moss (2 to 3 parts) with some added bark chips (1 part). Use more bark chips if light levels are expected to be on the lower side.

EXPECTATIONS

On average, anthuriums don't tend to hold as many active leaves as, say, philodendrons, but luckily their stems put out roots easily. This means as the older leaves die off (usually turning a bright yellow), there will be a bare stem with roots. You can mound up moist sphagnum moss around the stem to encourage root growth into the moss. Eventually, the moss mound will extend several inches above the top of the pot, at which time you can cut the stem and plant this mound with established roots into a new pot. The plant will be more comfortably seated lower into the new pot. The remaining stump can send up new shoots, though they will start off smaller than the leaves on the top cutting.

OPPOSITE LEFT: *Anthurium magnificum* with a prominent inflorescence from Benson's collection.

OPPOSITE RIGHT: Newly developing leaves on velvety anthuriums tend to have a reddish, bronze color—here's *Anthurium clarinervium* with a new leaf growing.

Anthurium growth expectations

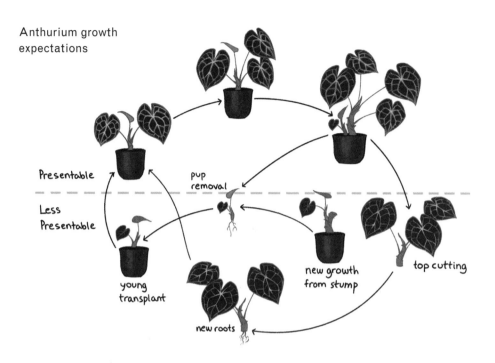

Presentable

Less Presentable

pup removal

young transplant

new growth from stump

top cutting

new roots

Anthurium Varieties to Collect

ABOVE LEFT: *Anthurium forgetii* has a rounder leaf that lacks a sinus (an indentation where the top of the leaf meets the petiole).

ABOVE RIGHT: Grace had an unrooted cutting of *Anthurium luxurians*. She rooted it into a substrate, and new leaves soon followed—nine months later the plant is spectacular!

RIGHT: Roos showing off her *Anthurium warocqueanum*, prized for its long, narrow foliage.

ABOVE LEFT AND RIGHT:
Tim gave me a tour of his collection, which is where I first encountered the *Anthurium veitchii* (above left). When I eventually got my own plant (above right), I learned to appreciate the transient nature of leaf perfection. Yes, higher humidity, soil flushing, and using distilled water may prolong the niceness of your active leaves, but I'm fine with just the one.

LEFT: *Anthurium plowmanii* shows another variation of leaf texture—ruffled edges.

Anthurium vittarifolium has long, strappy leaves that remind me of skinny ties. The emergent new leaves are VERY delicate—I've broken two or three from just handling the plant in the sink as I watered. I have to remind myself to be super careful when the next one comes around.

Observations of *Anthurium radicans*

Day 1

The *Anthurium radicans* is jokingly considered to be the poor man's *A. luxurians*. Despite the lower cost, I was still worried about the condition in which this plant arrived. I potted it into sphagnum moss and put it in my greenhouse cabinet.

1 month later

All the currently active leaves died off but the stump and roots looked firm and healthy. I didn't give up hope and just kept it in the cabinet.

2 months later

Signs of life! The first new leaf emerged one month after the dieback.

5 months later

The first few juvenile leaves still had some nice texture.

10 months later

The next set of leaves is noticeably bigger. The newest leaf begins with a deep red hue and gradually turns green as it hardens off.

Begonia

Begonias have been a longtime favorite of plant collectors because there are always new ones being created—they are readily hybridized to produce new cultivars. I'll show you two common forms of begonia that have very different growth patterns.

Cane begonias

The cane begonia develops a dark brown, woody stem that resembles a cane. The leaves of many cane-type begonias tend to have silvery spots and are wing-shaped, which gives us their common name, angel-wing begonia. There are also dragon-wing begonias. As the plant grows, the lowest leaves are continually shed. The total number of active leaves along the stem will reflect a combination of the growing environment and soil nutrition, but even with ideal conditions and care there will be some degree of lower leaf loss. Thankfully, cane begonias are easily propagated by stem cuttings.

OPPOSITE: Vanessa's collection of cane begonias.

Rhizomatous begonias

The main stem sends out leaves in a compact growth habit, giving the plant a nice, bushy look. Unlike cane begonias, which tend to grow upward, rhizomatous begonias crawl along the ground, so they tend to spread outward rather than grow taller. The familiar beefsteak begonia features leathery green leaves with red undersides. The Begonia Rex Cultorum varieties (rex begonias) are grown for their showy leaves with metallic colors and fascinating structures.

ABOVE: A selection of rhizomatous begonias in Tanya's collection.

ENVIRONMENT

Natural light: Indirect light levels in the 400–800 FC (80–160 µmol) will yield excellent growth but even 200–400 FC (40–80 µmol) is adequate. Tolerance for direct sun is dependent on the specific type of begonia. Thicker-leaved and cane begonias can tolerate 2–3 hours of direct sun but thin-leaved rhizomatous begonias do better without any direct sun.

Grow light: When you set your grow light so your rhizomatous begonia receives around 200 FC (40 µmol) for 12 hours, it should grow very well. The DLI will be 1.7 mol/day. For cane begonias, you can go higher, up to 800 FC (160 µmol) for 12 hours, which is DLI 6.9 mol/day.

Nursery light: Commercially produced begonias are grown with about 2,000 FC (400 µmol), which is 80 percent shade.

Temperature and Humidity: Begonias will grow with temperatures of 16–29 C (62–85 F) but will do best in the cooler range. Cane begonias do well in average room humidity (40–60 percent) while rhizomatous begonias (especially rexes) can benefit from a slightly higher range. Some begonias will grow best in a terrarium environment (60–80 percent humidity).

EFFORT

Watering: Cane begonias should be watered when the substrate is about halfway dry, but they tolerate short dry spells. If the plant is left too long without water, the leaves will shrivel up quickly. Rhizomatous begonias can also be watered when their soil is about halfway dry but err on the side of watering a bit sooner with thinner-leaved varieties. Rex begonias will wilt dramatically if their soil goes beyond halfway dry, so it is important to rehydrate before this occurs.

Fertilizing: A 3-1-2 or slow-release fertilizer added to the substrate will ensure good foliage growth.

Substrate: Standard potting soil (3 to 4 parts) with some added bark chips or perlite (1 part). If the drainage mixture is too high (meaning the substrate does not hold much water), you'll have to check the moisture level frequently.

EXPECTATIONS

Cane Begonia Long-Term Planning: The strategy for enjoying a cane begonia for the long term is to cut the stem back to the point where you want new growth to develop.

Sometimes there will already be an emergent spike along the stem. If you cut the stem above this growth point, it will become active. Although there will be a kink in the stem at the point where you made the cut, the new foliage should hide this. With excellent light, pups will form near the base of the stem. These can be removed and planted on their own or left with the rest of the plant to create a fuller-looking plant.

Rhizomatous Begonia Long-Term Planning: Over time, rhizomatous begonias keep growing longer rhizomes, dropping older leaves along the way. Eventually, the curvy rhizomes will grow out of the pot. You can cut back the top growth and root the cuttings in moist sphagnum moss to create a new plant. New shoots should also grow from the remaining rhizome.

Cane begonia growth
expectations

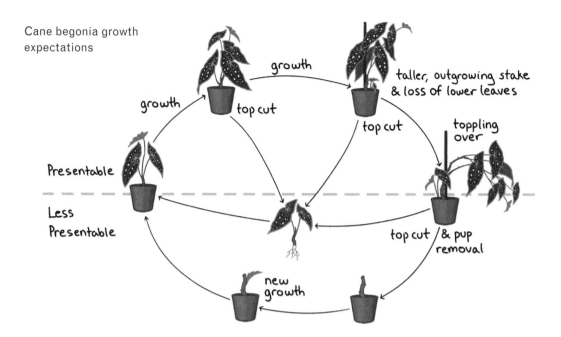

Rhizomatous begonia
growth expectations

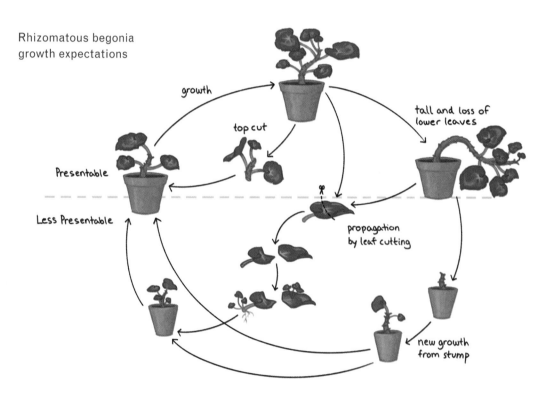

Propagating Cane Begonias

A cane begonia can tolerate a "hard pruning," meaning there are little to no leaves left on the plant—just bare stems. Here, 3 weeks after a hard pruning, the first new leaves on my Begonia 'Sophie Cecile' have finally emerged! Look how each cane has an obvious cut and continuation of growth. When more leaves have grown, they will conceal this kinked cane. In a plant with multiple canes, you can choose to cut back all the stems to near the soil line, essentially restarting the plant from the ground, or you can make staggered cuts so the overall plant will appear more full right from the first set of leaves. Here, I staggered the cuts.

I gifted the top cuttings from my Begonia 'Sophie Cecile' to a friend to propagate in water. Roots are forming.

5 months later, I'm a proud Begonia 'Sophie Cecile' collector! I'll enjoy the lush growth while it lasts . . . until the next pruning!

Meanwhile, 3 months after the hard pruning, the next set of leaves on my parent plant are larger and easily conceal the canes.

By the way, once a cane begonia gets to a certain height, the plant will need a vertical support from a bamboo stake or chopstick.

Propagating Rhizomatous Begonias from Leaf Segments

Rhizomatous begonias can be propagated by leaf segments. Using a clean, sharp blade, cut a healthy leaf with about an inch of the petiole, or leaf stalk, into two segments, as in this photo. New roots will emerge where you've exposed the leaf veins. Both the leaf blade and petiole segments can be propagated. Place the freshly cut leaf into a bed of moist sphagnum moss or perlite and seal in a container (clear clamshell food takeout containers are good for this). Make sure the cut side with the exposed veins is in contact with the moist substrate. Only 1-2 mol/day is necessary in terms of light—this can be achieved with a grow light measuring 100-200 FC (20-40 µmol) for 12 hours/day (works out to 0.9-1.7 mol/day).

Here, 6 weeks later, new leaves have emerged from the base of the old leaf, while new roots have grown in the sphagnum moss. Once the new plants are about an inch tall, transplant them to individual pots (2- or 3-inch diameter) and keep them in a humidity dome. Check on the substrate moisture and ensure it does not fully dry out—you can mist it occasionally.

When they outgrow their small pots, the plants can be transplanted to the next size up and grown at ambient humidity. The original leaf was starting to fade 3 months after transplanting, so I removed it from the main plant, which has filled in the pot nicely.

Cane Begonia Varieties to Collect

TOP LEFT: Begonia 'Corallina de Lucerna' is a hybrid between *B. teuscheri* and *B. coccinea*—the plant belongs to Beverly, who has been growing it since 1978. This angel-wing hybrid has been popular for more than a century.

LEFT: *Begonia maculata* var. *wightii*, the polka-dot begonia.

TOP RIGHT: Begonia 'Miss Mummy'—the metallic pink foliage will grow best with strong light (200–400 FC most of the day).

ABOVE: Begonia 'Cracklin' Rosie' features deep green leaves with pinkish spots.

Rhizomatous Begonia Varieties to Collect

OPPOSITE: Begonia 'Gryphon'—although this begonia grows rather cane-like, it can propagate by leaf cutting, which is a trait of rhizomatous begonias.

TOP ROW: Begonia 'Erythrophylla' is a very popular rhizomatous begonia, commonly called beefsteak begonia. Three freshly propagated top cuttings (left) grew into a nice bushy plant (right) in about a year. The plant lived in a south window, getting direct sun for about 2 hours while the rest of the day, the indirect light levels were in the 200–400 FC (40–80 µmol) range. A nice set of flower stalks have also emerged!

BOTTOM ROW: Begonia 'Tiger Kitten' plants (left) are ready for sale. A plantlet developing from leaf propagation (right).

A Few Humidity-Loving Begonias to Collect

THIS PAGE: Once you have dedicated space for a higher-humidity environment, there are many more begonias to collect and enjoy. Planting several begonias together into a terrarium creates an interesting display. A terrarium is surprisingly low maintenance once planted—I haven't added water to this one for two months and the sphagnum moss is still moist! It sits near a grow light, receiving about 200 FC (40 µmol) for 12 hours a day.

TOP LEFT: Begonia 'Dinhdui' has a metallic quality.

TOP RIGHT: *Begonia natunaensis*—this species of rhizomatous begonia is native to Borneo.

BOTTOM LEFT: *Begonia dracopelta* with bullate (bumpy) leaf texture.

BOTTOM RIGHT: *Begonia quadrialata* ssp. *Nimbaensis*—this subspecies is prized for its reddish veins.

Calathea/Goeppertia/Ctenanthe

Calatheas have long been appreciated for their boldly pat-
terned leaves with their appealing habit of closing at night.
Like other plants in our time of DNA sequencing, many
species in the genus *Calathea* were moved to the genus
Goeppertia in 2012. Plants in the genus *Ctenanthe*, in the
same family, have similarly showy leaves and growing
requirements. For the purpose of discussing their care, it's
fine to think of them all as "calatheas."

Calatheas, freshly grown and groomed (meaning any dying leaves have been clipped off) in the nursery, are a typical first-time plant purchase on account of their striking appearance, but their notoriously short leaf life span often leads to disappointment. It seems to be an inevitable cycle: Buy the attractive calathea, get browned tips, lose interest in caring for the plant, discard. Or for the persevering: Struggle to maintain high humidity, use only distilled water, delay the inevitable. My advice: Accept that these amazing leaves have a limited life span and enjoy calatheas for as long as they remain presentable to you.

OPPOSITE: Higher humidity won't keep leaves perfect forever! Plants in this collection: *Goeppertia insignis* (top left), *Goeppertia roseopicta* (right), and *Ctenanthe burle-marxii* (bottom left).

ENVIRONMENT

Natural light: Indirect light levels in the 200–400 FC (40–80 μmol) range will yield excellent growth, while just 100–200 FC (20–40 μmol) is sufficient. Direct sun can be tolerated for just an hour or two, beyond which leaves will fade over time.

Grow light: Set your grow light to deliver about 200 FC (40 μmol) for 12 hours (this is DLI 1.7 mol/day).

Nursery light: Commercial production of calathea is achieved with 80–90 percent shade, which is 1,000–2,000 FC most of the day.

Temperature and Humidity: Calathea will grow with temperatures of 21–32 C (70–90 F) but will do best in the cooler range. Most calathea can grow well in average room humidity (40–60 percent), but leaf quality can be prolonged at higher humidity (60–80 percent). Higher levels of humidity are recommended for calathea because rapid transpiration in less humid environments causes minerals from the soil to accumulate and the cells in those tips to die off. Humidity is an environmental factor that's hard to control in large open spaces, so if you're a perfectionist, you may want to keep your calathea collection in a greenhouse cabinet and flush the soil regularly. Leaf browning will still set in eventually, because it's inevitable as hairs turning gray. It is simply the fact of leaf life.

EFFORT

Watering: Calatheas prefer evenly moist soil, so they should be watered before the substrate reaches halfway dry. While drought tolerance varies by the variety, all calatheas display signs of extreme thirst when the outer edges of their leaves curl inward. Should this happen, it's time for a thorough watering. Most calatheas will recover from this kind of wilting, but the situation should be avoided by keeping on top of watering.

Fertilizing: A 3-1-2 fertilizer or a slow-release fertilizer added to the substrate will ensure good foliage growth.

Substrate: Standard potting soil (3 to 4 parts) with some added bark chips or perlite (1 part). If the drainage mixture is too high (meaning the substrate does not hold much water), you'll have to check the moisture level frequently.

EXPECTATIONS

I cannot stress this idea enough, especially with calatheas: Leaves have a limited life span, which means the way to enjoy calatheas in the long term is to give them adequate light and consistent moisture, and the growth of new leaves should balance the death of old ones. New plants can be propagated by division.

ABOVE: Here's a VERY thirsty *Ctenanthe burle-marxii* 'Amagris'. Although you should avoid letting your plant get to this stage of dryness, it can recover with a thorough soaking.

Calathea Varieties to Collect

ABOVE LEFT AND RIGHT: *Goeppertia insignis (Calathea lancifolia)*—with good light and fertilizing, the rate of leaf turnover shouldn't be too upsetting, as this plant maintains a good number of active leaves (left). Although all calatheas exhibit some form of daily leaf movement, the lancifolia looks quite bundled up at night (right), such that a new owner might wonder if something is wrong. Don't be alarmed. This is the usual cycle of leaf movement.

LEFT: *Ctenanthe burle-marxii*—not only attractive but very durable and long-lasting. The leaf loss rate is offset by lots of new growth in good conditions. And high humidity is optional, as this species grows well even in dry winter indoor conditions.

ABOVE: *Goeppertia makoyana*—commonly known as "peacock plant."

TOP RIGHT: *Ctenanthe oppenheimiana*—the foliage can reach two or three feet tall, which makes it a good floor plant.

BOTTOM RIGHT: *Goeppertia roseopicta* 'Medallion'—I decided to dress in the green/purple color theme. Because the *G. roseopicta* grows larger but fewer leaves (it's not as densely foliated as, say, the *G. insignis*), the leaf turnover can feel more alarming.

Observations on *Calathea musaica* 'Network'

My friend Melissa got a large Calathea 'Network' and I was pleasantly surprised by how well it grew near a large patio door, getting a few hours of direct sun and indirect light in the 400–800 FC range. The plant eventually filled its pot, so she let me take a piece by root division.

Using a sharp knife, I cut a small section—roughly a quarter of the root-ball—and potted up both pieces into separate pots.

After another few months, dozens of new leaves started emerging like a bunch of little trumpets.

18 months since repotting

When we unpotted the plant, we found the root system had formed a tough barrier in the shape of its pot.

For the first few months, my plant looked slightly awkward and sparse, but I kept it well lit (grow light at 200 FC for 12 hours) and fertilized (using a liquid 3-1-2 fertilizer at every watering).

I let the plant live outside behind my shaded pergola, where it received about 1 hour of direct sun while the dappled and indirect light hovered in the 400–800 FC (80–160 µmol) range. The new leaves have filled in so nicely!

Observations on *Goeppertia orbifolia*

Day 1

A gift from a local plant shop! I was excited to start with a small plant (4-inch pot) to see it grow. (By the way, this species was recently reclassified from *Calathea orbifolia* to *Goeppertia orbifolia*— either way, it's the same plant.)

2 months

Happy to report new leaf progress. The rolled-up leaves keep emerging from the center of the group of stems, each one bigger and more fabulous than the previous. The light situation so far: The plant got 200–300 FC (around 40–60 µmol) of indirect light most of the day. The sun did not shine directly on the plant. Watering the plant with 3-1-2 fertilizer at every watering whenever the soil was partially dry seemed to keep new leaves coming.

2.5 months

The first leaf loss. This was one of the smallest and oldest leaves, so I was not concerned. At this stage of yellowing, the leaf was easily pulled off—thank you for your service!

Instead of blindly trying to raise humidity in an effort to preserve leaf perfection, measure it! My indoor humidity gets to 40–50 percent in the fall and 30–40 percent in the winter. So long as I have ensured that light levels are good and that I am watering/fertilizing accordingly, I am quite pleased with the growth of my calathea and other allegedly "humidity-loving" plants like the maidenhair fern.

10 months

After discovering a mealybug infestation, the constant picking and spraying was becoming too much of a hassle. I decided to cut off all leaves except one. Discarding the majority of the plant severely decreased the mealybug population, while the goal of leaving just the one leaf was to lure any lingering mealybugs to where I could easily monitor them.

Large adult mealybugs are easy to see and kill . . .

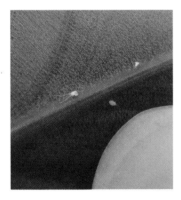

. . . but remember to take out the smaller larvae that easily evade detection. You can use a small piece of tape to physically lift off all the bugs in a small area and follow up with an insecticidal soap spraying.

When a plant has been receiving adequate light, all that work (photosynthesis) creates stockpiles of carbohydrates that are stored in the roots. If you suddenly cut off its leaves, the plant will use that stockpile of energy to produce new leaves. The new leaf spikes are a good sign!

11 months

A difficulty I had not anticipated was mealybugs hanging out inside the rolled up new leaves. As much

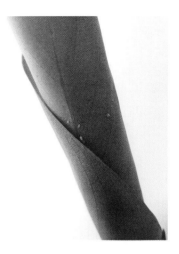

as I am careful to not damage the new leaf, there are some areas that a cotton swab simply cannot reach.

14 months
I'm very happy with the new growth over the past few months while keeping the mealybugs under control. Juvenile leaves start out small (roughly the size of my palm) and subsequent leaves can become quite a bit larger with good growing conditions. The edges of the leaves are susceptible to browning—occasionally flushing the soil can slow this process.

Ceropegia

The commonly available *Ceropegia woodii*—string/chain of hearts or rosary vine—has different varieties that are fun to collect, along with a few other ceropegia species. Given their appeal as multiple dangling strands, you'll have to propagate your plants in order to keep your collection looking lush. Note that string-of-pearls (*Curio rowleyanus*), with pea-like globular leaves, is an entirely different plant, also fun (if challenging) to grow.

OPPOSITE: Cyril's collection drapes down from a second-story landing—the middle plants all being from the *Ceropegia* genus.

ENVIRONMENT

Natural light: You should get adequate growth if your average indirect light is above 100 FC (20 µmol), but the plant will do much better in the 400–800 FC range (80–160 µmol). With adequate watering, ceropegia can tolerate 2–3 hours of direct sun. Use a white sheer curtain to diffuse the sun if the duration of direct exposure will be longer.

Grow light: Set up your grow light so that the ceropegia will receive at least 200 FC (40 µmol) for 12 hours/day (equivalent to DLI 1.7 mol/day) for good growth.

Nursery light: Ceropegia are produced with 60–70 percent shade, which translates to around 3,000–4,000 FC (600–800 µmol) most of the day.

Temperature and Humidity: Ceropegia will grow well with daily temperatures in the 21–29 C (70–85 F) range. Average room humidity (40–60 percent) is suitable for good growth.

EFFORT

Watering: Water a ceropegia when its substrate is almost completely dry. These plants are quite drought tolerant as they store water in underground tubers. With prolonged dryness, the leaves will become thin and pliable—be sure to water thoroughly if the plant reaches this point.

Fertilizing: A fertilizer with NPK ratio 3-1-2 will be suitable.

Substrate: Ceropegia prefer a well-draining substrate, similar to cactus soil. Use 2 or 3 parts coco coir or peat moss with 1 part coarse sand or perlite.

EXPECTATIONS

Ceropegia vines will keep getting longer as they lose older leaves—the first ones to go will be those near the soil. If you wish to fill in these bald areas, you can take vine cuttings, root them in water or a propagation box, then transplant them once the new roots are about 1 cm long. You can perpetually propagate a ceropegia in this way to maintain the plant's lushness.

Ceropegia Varieties to Collect

TOP LEFT AND RIGHT: *Ceropegia woodii* can grow relatively quickly in modest light (200–400 FC most of the day, left). Look at the plant 7 months later (right)!

BOTTOM RIGHT: The variegated *C. woodii* features cream-colored leaf margins and slightly lighter purple backsides. Here are some plants being propagated for sale.

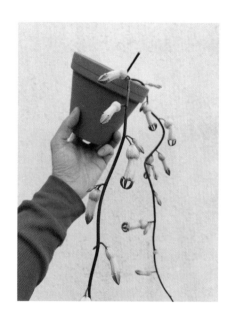

TOP LEFT: *Ceropegia ampliata* ("bushman's pipe")—not all of the ceropegia species form strings. This one produces some rather unique-looking flowers, like ornaments on a strange Christmas tree.

BOTTOM LEFT: *Ceropegia simoneae* 'Green Bizarre'—reminds me of a dragon! The light and watering parameters are succulent-like.

TOP RIGHT AND ABOVE: *Ceropegia sandersonii*— the leaves aren't all that interesting, but the flowers (above) are special and give the species its common name: parachute plant.

OPPOSITE: This is Melissa's *Ceropegia woodii* 'Silver Glory'. When the plant is adequately lit, the silver will be most pronounced.

Dieffenbachia

The dieffenbachia is well-loved for its showy leaves and upright growth habit. Larger varieties make great statement plants in a floor container. Smaller plants fit nicely on tables or shelves. Care should be taken not to ingest the plant, as it produces calcium oxalates, which are toxic to animals and people—it can cause paralysis of the mouth, which is how this plant got its common but derogatory name, "dumb cane."

ABOVE: Most dieffenbachias grow anywhere from a large table plant (6-inch pot) to floor height (12-inch pot or larger), so you may not have space to collect more than a half dozen or so. Varieties shown here: Dieffenbachia 'Honeydew' (bottom left), *D. maculata* 'Tropic Tiki' (top left), D. 'Sterling' (center), and D. 'Panther' (right).

ENVIRONMENT

Natural light: As an understory plant, a dieffenbachia will grow well with indirect light above 200 FC (40 µmol), but the plant will do much better in the 400–800 FC (80–160 µmol) range. With adequate watering, dieffenbachia can tolerate 2–3 hours of direct sun. Use a white sheer curtain to diffuse the sun if the duration of direct exposure will be longer.

Grow light: A diffenbachia should receive at least 200 FC (40 µmol) for 12 hours/day (equivalent to DLI 1.7 mol/day) for good growth.

Nursery light: Commercial production of dieffenbachia is done with 80 percent shade, which is 2,000 FC (400 µmol) and lasts most of the day.

Temperature and Humidity: Dieffenbachia will grow best in the temperature range of 18–26 C (65–80 F) and average room humidity (30–50 percent).

EFFORT

Watering: Allow the dieffenbachia's substrate to reach about halfway to three-quarters dry before watering. The plant can tolerate spells of total dryness, but growth will be stunted.

Fertilizing: A fertilizer with NPK ratio of 3-1-2 or slow-release fertilizer added to the substrate will work.

Substrate: Standard potting soil (2 to 3 parts) with some added perlite or bark chips (1 part). Using bark chips instead of perlite is useful for filling up a larger pot (larger than 12 inches).

EXPECTATIONS

With each growth spurt of new leaves, there will be a roughly similar number of lower leaves that drop off, and the plant will eventually assume an awkward structure: Leaves at the top and a long, bare stem. In the wild, the stem would simply bend until it reaches the ground and, if the conditions are right, new roots will form. In your home, such long stems may become unruly, making propagation a sensible option to reset the plant. You can air layer the top portion of the plant, or simply cut it off and get it to root in moist sphagnum moss or water. Pieces of the stem can be cut into chonks (leafless nodes) and laid sideways in moist sphagnum moss. Keep the moss evenly moist and in a few weeks or months, a new growth point will emerge, forming a new plant. You can also do this in a clear, closed container and you won't have to moisten the moss as often. New pups can also emerge from the soil, and they can be removed and planted on their own.

Dieffenbachia Varieties to Collect

LEFT: Dieffenbachia 'Camille' (left) and D. 'Sparkles' (right). I only include Camille so I can report that every time I get a "what's wrong with my plant?" question related dieffenbachia, it's always a Camille. This must be a popular cultivar, and it's probably being grown too far from any windows and under-fertilized. Within a few weeks, most of the lower leaves will have fallen off and, due to poor lighting and nutrition, the new growth is slow or nonexistent.

OPPOSITE TOP LEFT AND RIGHT: Dieffenbachia 'Crocodile'—a leaf mutation causes this interesting texture along the back of the midrib.

OPPOSITE BOTTOM LEFT: Dieffenbachia 'Camouflage' has speckled light green foliage.

OPPOSITE BOTTOM RIGHT: Dieffenbachia 'Panther'—the lighter blotches are part of the plant; it's not a disease!

Observations of *Dieffenbachia seguine* 'Tropic Snow'

My friend's parents owned a Chinese restaurant where they kept a lovely *Dieffenbachia seguine* 'Tropic Snow' to greet incoming guests. With the sun shining directly onto the front window and the plant a few feet back, the indirect light was in the 200–400 FC (roughly 40–80 µmol) range most of the day. Every few years, with the sprouting of new leaves at the top and corresponding lower leaves dropping off, the owners do a kind of air layering technique.

Day 1

They cut a tin can and secured it around the lower part of the trunk and filled it with soil. Air layering usually involves "injuring" the stem by partially cutting into it, but this wasn't necessary in this case.

4 months

They uprooted the whole plant and severed the stem section that was covered by the can—it was already sending out new growth.

They kept the rooted top-cutting and gave me the stump, which I potted into a 16-inch pot.

Day 1 since potting

Seeing the size of the mother plant, I had no doubts that this cutting would fill up the pot in good time!

5 months since potting

Good growth of the three stems while living in the upstairs hallway of my parents' home. Light source: skylight. The diffused light from the skylight measures in the 200–400 FC range. For roughly 1 hour in the afternoon, the sun comes into direct line of sight, which yields ~4,000 FC.

10 months since potting

The volume of foliage has now balanced nicely with the pot, creating a lovely specimen plant.

Moving with plants

I tend to treat them like people rather than furniture!

14 months since potting

Inevitable leaf loss. The light you have is the light you have; do your best with watering and fertilizing and let nature take its course. The oldest leaves will eventually retire. If the growing conditions and care were good, the plant would have grown many new leaves by the time older ones fell.

You might have heard that cutting off a leaf at the first sign of yellowing saves the plant energy for newer leaves. Not true. Even with good fertilizing habits, there will be a limit to the total number of leaves that the plant can hold at any given time. As the plant utilizes available nutrients (mostly nitrogen) to make new leaves, the older leaf is signaled to break down its cellular components that can be salvaged—the mobile nutrients. If you want to do what's best for the plant, leave the yellowing leaf until it is completely yellow before cutting it off. In some cases, it will come off with a gentle tug. Each line on the trunk of this plant is the scar of a fallen leaf—this is how the plant grows. If you find the yellowing unsightly, then cutting it off immediately will not have a significant impact on the future growth of the plant. Just don't tell yourself you're doing the plant a favor!

2 years since repotting

The plant is now at its optimal size in terms of the balance between lush foliage and pot size (and this is completely subjective—whatever looks good to you!).

Echeveria and Other Small Succulents

Echeverias, with their multitude of pastel tones and neat rosette growth habit, have always enchanted collectors. In the wild, as animals brush past the plant, the thick leaves get knocked to the ground, which helps to start a new plant. You might witness this at home as you discover a fallen leaf growing a new rosette.

There's nothing like a lovely succulent arrangement to adorn a dining table, but all too often the plants end up looking sad and are quietly thrown away. It doesn't have to be this way! You might think that with "proper care," a bowl of perfect succulents will remain that way forever. Reality check: They won't stay that way no matter how good your care is, so you should expect to do a reset every few years or so.

OPPOSITE TOP: Succulents come in a range of colors that are rare in other plants.

OPPOSITE BOTTOM: Serious hobbyists like Vivian have multiple shelves with long LED grow lights attached to the bottom of each shelf. If you like "neat and tidy," you could have hundreds of echeverias lined up in an orderly fashion.

ENVIRONMENT

Natural light: Three to four hours of direct sun would be ideal. For the rest of the day, indirect light at 400 FC (80 μmol) is sufficient, but better growth will occur above 800 FC (160 μmol). Truthfully, this is difficult to achieve unless you have a very large, unobstructed window.

Grow light: Aim for a DLI range of 4–10 mol/day; 8.6 mol/day can be achieved with 1,000 FC (200 μmol) for 12 hours. Slightly slower development will occur at lower light levels, such as 600 FC (120 μmol) for 12 hours, which is 5.2 mol/day.

Nursery light: Most succulents are produced with light levels of 3,000–5,000 FC (approximately 50–70 percent shade).

Temperature and Humidity: Most succulents will grow well in temperatures of 21–32 C (70–90 F) and dry to average room humidity (20–60 percent).

EFFORT

Watering: The thing most people say about succulents and watering is "they hardly need water, right?" While it is true that rain is infrequent in an arid environment, when it does rain, it pours. Assuming that the planting medium is suitable for the succulent, when it is time to water, you should thoroughly and evenly soak all parts of the soil. Because the soil will be highly draining, it is best to water in a sink or even fully submerge the pot in water. The cue to water is when the soil is completely dry.

Fertilizing: Any 3-1-2 fertilizer will be suitable for succulents.

Substrate: The first thought for succulents is usually "add drainage," but be sure you consider the light levels in your setup. If the substrate drains too quickly and you are working in the higher light range (say 20 mol/day), you might be watering very frequently to keep up with "when completely dry." In high light, you could safely go with 3 parts coir/peat moss and 1 part coarse sand/perlite. In more modest light, the mixture can be as low as 2 or 1 part coir/peat moss to 1 part coarse sand/perlite. For smaller root systems and smaller pots (less than 3 inches in diameter), using coarse sand may help to anchor the plant better, since perlite has a larger particle size than sand.

ABOVE: A nursery setting where succulents are produced.

Echeveria growth
expectations

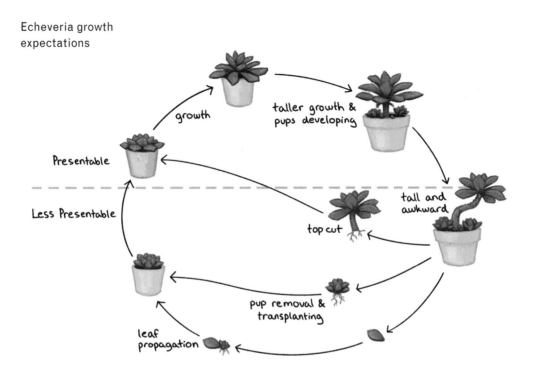

growth

taller growth &
pups developing

Presentable

- -

Less Presentable

tall and
awkward

top cut

pup removal &
transplanting

leaf
propagation

EXPECTATIONS

The secret to eternal succulent life is propagation. The plant you originally bought will eventually grow leggy—sooner with less light. Experienced succulent growers know the cycle of succulent life:

- "Perfect rosette" (1–2 years with good light; a few months with poor light).
- Plant becomes tall and awkward.
- Cut off the top and transplant it to soil (1–2 months to establish roots).
- Propagate the lower leaves (3–6 months to make small plants).

What happens if you do nothing? The tip will continue growing well beyond the pot, and the plant may eventually fall over. While you can certainly leave it this way, the plant will be more manageable if kept smaller. But you may also enjoy the unique character of a trailing succulent.

TOP ROW: Echeveria 'Blue Bird'—most of the lower leaves have died off (left). Time to remove them and take a top cutting (right). This can be planted directly into a suitable succulent substrate. Moisten the substrate whenever it is partially dry and, in a few weeks, it should take root.

BOTTOM ROW: Succulent leaf propagation: The month-old leaf cuttings being moistened (left) are starting to form roots. They received about 800 FC for 12 hours a day and sat on a heat mat, which raised the soil temperature to around 30 C (86 F). Six months later (right), the rosettes have fully formed

and the original leaves used for propagation have withered away. The plant is Echeveria 'Perle von Nürnberg', known for its gentle purple/blue leaves, which become more intense with higher light—you might even get some red tips.

Echeveria Varieties to Collect

ABOVE: *Echeveria nodulosa* is commonly called "painted echeveria" because of the burgundy stripes on its leaves. This plant is getting quite tall and sending out a pup. Unless you want a floppy plant, it's definitely time for propagation and a reset!

RIGHT: *Echeveria runyonii* 'Topsy Turvy' has a smooth blue-green color with upward curved leaves.

TOP: Echeveria 'Marble' has some uniquely textured leaves that you may misinterpret as a thirsty plant!

BOTTOM: Variegation tends to command higher prices, and succulents are no different. Here's Echeveria 'Japan Moon River' variegata.

Other Small Succulents to Collect

TOP LEFT: *Adromischus marianiae herrei*—this specimen has grown to the point where top cuttings could be taken.

TOP RIGHT: Boobie cactus (*Myrtillocactus geometrizans* cv. *Fukurokuryuzinboku*)—like many succulents that adopt dwarf habits in the home, this plant can grow to be taller than you are in nature.

BOTTOM LEFT: Despite their dramatically different structures, these four plants are all in the *Euphorbia* genus! Front left and right: *E. obesa* and *E. decaryi*. Rear left and right: *E. platyclada* and *E. x japonica*.

BOTTOM MIDDLE: Crassula 'Buddha's Temple'—several pups have developed from this plant. In a few weeks, they can be separated into individual pots and the top of this plant can be cut and replanted.

Epipremnum

Epipremnum aureum, or pothos, is in the same subfamily as the monsteras and has an equally long history as a popular house plant. I covered the basics of pothos care in *The New Plant Parent*, but if you're looking for a rewarding challenge with a readily available plant, try your hand at growing one up a moss pole. Do it well and you'll be rewarded with huge leaves as the plant climbs up! Most house plants you will find in the genus *Epipremnum* are cultivars of *E. aureum*, but varieties of *E. pinnatum* are also interesting.

OPPOSITE: Jainey's collection of moss-pole cultivated plants includes the pothos, monsteras, and philodendrons shown here.

ENVIRONMENT

Natural light: For excellent growth, find a large enough window to get indirect light close to 400 FC (80 µmol). Two or three hours of direct sun is tolerable, but you should be vigilant about checking the soil moisture—use a diffusing material if direct sun will exceed three hours.

Grow light: 400 FC (80 µmol) for 12 hours/day will provide a DLI of 3.5 mol/day, which should be sufficient.

Nursery light: Epipremnum are commercially produced at 2,000–3,000 FC (70–80 percent shade).

Temperature and Humidity: Epipremnum will grow best in the temperature range of 18–29 C (65–85 F) and average room humidity (30–50 percent). The more delicate-leaved epipremnum varieties will do better with higher humidity (60–80 percent).

EFFORT

Watering: Water when the substrate is partially dry. Epipremnum are drought tolerant, so they can recover from a dry spell, but their growth will be stunted.

Fertilizing: A fertilizer with NPK ratio 3-1-2 will work well for epipremnum. A liquid or slow-release fertilizer can be used.

Substrate: Standard potting soil (2 to 3 parts) with some added perlite or bark chips (1 part). Use more drainage material if light levels are expected to be on the lower side.

EXPECTATIONS (MOSS POLE TECHNIQUE)

You can always maintain a trailing epipremnum by trimming the vines and making top and node cuttings, but try growing one on a pole for a different look. The pole needs to be filled with a medium that retains moisture so that the nodes can send roots into the moss. Sphagnum moss, which is like a string of little sponges, is best. One typical method of making a moss pole is to roll a piece of plastic fencing mesh (available at most hardware stores or garden centers) into a cylinder that you can fill with the moist moss. Then fasten it closed with zip ties. Depending on the size of your pole, you might want to stiffen it with a dowel or plastic garden stake.

The great thing about this project: you only need ONE vine to get started!

Patience is key. While it might be tempting to give your climber a head start by taking a long cutting, simply pressing the vine into the moss will not cause the current juvenile leaves to get any bigger. These leaves have already reached their full size. Instead, you must start with a new growth point. As that new vine sends out new leaves and nodes, gradually tie them against the moss pole.

Each new leaf develops its shape and structure based on the orientation and root status of the previous leaves. It's as if they tell the newly developing leaf: "Hey, things are looking up and there's a good source of moisture so keep growing in that direction!"

Epipremnum growth
expectations

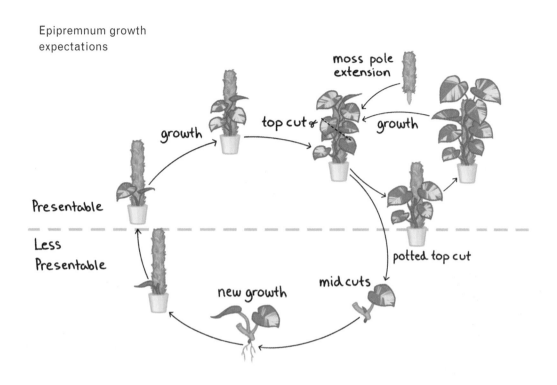

moss pole
extension

growth

top cut

growth

Presentable

Less
Presentable

potted top cut

new growth

mid cuts

LEFT: I kept an *Epipremnum aureum* 'Marble Queen' on my balcony during the summer months. The leaves that grew during that time have a much richer cream color, resulting in more striking variegation, as in the last 5–6 leaves on the vine. The older leaves that grew indoors have slightly less contrast and look a bit dull in comparison to the leaves that grew outdoors. You might say both grew with "bright indirect light," but with more detailed measurement, I found that the outdoor indirect light levels were in the 400–800 FC range (80–160 µmol), as opposed to 100–200 FC (20–40 µmol) for the indoor levels.

Transplanting an *Epipremnum aureum* 'Marble Queen'

Jainey's 'Marble Queen' is showing some noticeably larger leaves toward the top of the moss pole.

As the vines have reached the top of the pole, Jainey decided it was time to cut the pole and make two plants. The great thing about moss pole cuttings is that the plant is already rooted into the moss on the pole. The upper section can be potted up with some extra moss around the base of the pole, and the plant will root into its new pot. Both poles can be extended to allow for new top growth.

1 month since cutting

Maintaining the moisture on a moss pole poses a few challenges when working in an indoor space. The easiest way would be to bring the whole contraption outside or into a bathtub where you can shower it liberally. Once it has stopped dripping, you can return it to its grow space. Alternatively, you could fill a small plastic bottle with water and put it upside down at the top of the pole, allowing the water to percolate through the moss. Lastly, here's one of the rare occasions where I would recommend misting as a way to deliver moisture directly to the moss pole with minimal wetting of the floors.

Epipremnum Varieties to Collect

Epipremnum pinnatum variegata—leaves get progressively larger when supported. Some fenestrations can be seen on newer leaves.

THIS PAGE: *Epipremnum aureum* 'Manjula' features dark green margins with spotted cream colors in the center. Some of the more exotic pothos plants are sold as a single vine—Natasha's plant is just starting its journey (top left). Good growth from this single vine after 6 months (top right). After a few rounds of propagation, the plant has filled the pot nicely a year later (left).

OPPOSITE TOP ROW: *Epipremnum pinnatum* 'Skeleton Key'—these cuttings (left) have rooted nicely in water and are ready to be potted up. I will give them a moss pole in the hopes of leveling up the new leaves. A few months later, the vines have taken to the moss pole (right)!

OPPOSITE BOTTOM ROW: *Epipremnum pinnatum* 'Cebu Blue': Getting a few cuttings from friends is always a treat (left). A year later, the vines are ready to become more propagations (right). The slight blueish tone of this cultivar comes through on mature leaves.

Ferns

Ferns are, evolutionarily speaking, older than flowering plants. Instead of reproducing by flowers and seeds, ferns produce spores, which are dispersed by wind and rain. In the right conditions, the spores develop into full-grown ferns. Ferns have a compact growth habit, developing into a nice shrub-like structure emerging from a central rosette. Many of the ferns that are fun to collect are epiphytic, growing on rocks or trees.

OPPOSITE: Three kinds of maidenhair ferns—left to right in the palm of my hand: *Adiantum microphyllum* has the smallest leaves, *Adiantum raddianum* or Delta maidenhair fern is a popular house plant, and *Adiantum peruvianum* or silver-dollar maidenhair fern, which has the largest leaves.

ENVIRONMENT

Natural light: You should get adequate growth if your average indirect light is above 100 FC (20 µmol), but the plant will do much better in the 400–800 FC range (80–160 µmol). Most ferns can tolerate 1–2 hours of direct sun, but it is critical to keep up with watering. Use a white sheer curtain to diffuse the sun if the duration of direct exposure will be longer.

Grow light: Ferns should receive at least 200 FC (40 µmol) for 12 hours/day for good growth (equivalent to DLI 1.7 mol/day).

Nursery light: 90 percent shade is used to produce most ferns, which translates to around 1,000 FC most of the day.

Temperature and Humidity: Ferns will grow well with daily temperatures in the 16–27 C (60–80 F) range. Most will grow well with average room humidity (40–60 percent) but your task of keeping up with watering will be slightly easier with higher humidity (60–80 percent).

EFFORT

Watering: Thin-leaved ferns should be kept evenly moist at all times—this is especially true of the maidenhair fern. Ferns with thicker leaves and prominent rhizomes are better at tolerating drought and can be watered when the substrate is about halfway dry.

Fertilizing: A fertilizer with NPK ratio 3-1-2 will be suitable.

Substrate: Standard potting soil (3 to 4 parts) with some added perlite or bark chips (1 part). In higher light conditions, you can omit the extra perlite/bark chips: The higher water retention will offset the more rapid water usage.

RIGHT: Here's why "consistent moisture" can trump "avoid direct sun" where ferns are concerned: Maidenhair ferns thrive where the water drains from an alley, even with a few hours of direct sun exposure.

EXPECTATIONS

If you start with a small specimen, a 4-inch pot for instance, you could go up a pot size about once year as the plant keeps filling up the new space. Eventually, you can divide the roots to create two smaller plants. Note that ferns will not propagate from cuttings of the fronds, but cuttings taken from the rhizomes of rhizomatous ferns will root.

For ferns that grow from a central point, the long-term plan is to continually cut off the oldest, outermost leaves, as new ones grow from the center. You may see new pups emerging from the soil next to your main plant—these can be removed and potted on their own once they are big enough to comfortably fit in a small pot.

Fern Varieties to Collect

TOP LEFT: *Davallia fejeensis* or rabbit's foot fern. I repotted mine into a ceramic bowl with sphagnum moss. Although there was no drainage hole, I was confident that the light would be strong enough to drive timely water usage. Here's the plant after two years.

TOP RIGHT: Ant ferns are named for their symbiotic relationship with ants in the wild. The rhizomes have tunnels so ants can take up residence, providing the fern with nutrients (in the form of ant waste) in exchange for shelter. Left: *Lecanopteris lomariodes*—the rhizomes have a furry texture. Right: *Lecanopteris deparioides*—some truly alien-looking rhizomes.

BOTTOM LEFT: An assortment of ferns with particularly interesting fronds waiting for a shower. Front row: *Microsorum thailandicum* or cobalt fern (left) and *Asplenium nidus* 'Crissie' (right); back row, *Asplenium antiquum* 'Lasagna' or lasagna fern (left) and *Asplenium nidus* 'Osaka' (right).

BOTTOM RIGHT: *Microsorum thailandicum* or cobalt fern has stiff metallic fronds with an iridescent quality, reflecting green and blue in certain kinds of light.

Haworthia/Haworthiopsis

Haworthia is an amazing genus to collect—there are dozens of species and hybrids available. They grow in a compact form so they can be kept for several years in a small space. As they grow, pups emerge near the base of the plant, forming a clump, which you can easily separate and give to friends or just keep the entire clump for yourself.

They originated from southern Africa and naturally grow in arid, rocky crevices with infrequent rainfall. In cultivation, protected from the harshness of the wild, haworthia show off their fascinating leaf structures and characteristics.

Recent genetic studies have split off a group of plants that were once all considered part of the genus *Haworthia*. Haworthiopsis have tough leaves with white, bumpy markings while haworthia have smooth leaves with some translucent areas. People will probably still refer to all these plants as haworthia—and for the purposes of care, they are generally the same.

OPPOSITE: Dave's collection of (true) haworthia: Notice the translucent leaf tips.

ENVIRONMENT

Natural light: Three to four hours of direct sun would be ideal. For the rest of the day, indirect light at 200 FC (40 µmol) is sufficient, but better growth will occur above 400 FC (80 µmol).

Grow light: With a grow light providing around 400 FC (80 µmol) for 12 hours, you will get a DLI of 3.5 mol/day, which will yield good growth from haworthia.

Nursery light: 3,000–5,000 FC (approximately 50–70 percent shade) will work well for haworthia.

Temperature and Humidity: Haworthia will grow well in temperatures of 21–32 C (70–90 F) and dry to average room humidity (20–60 percent).

EFFORT

Watering: Water when the substrate is completely dry. With prolonged dryness, some haworthia will be noticeably less plump. After a thorough watering, the plant will recover.

Fertilizing: Any 3-1-2 fertilizer will be suitable for haworthia.

Substrate: Similar to most succulents, the substrate can be 2 or 1 part coir/peat moss to 1 part coarse sand/perlite. If working in higher light, you could increase the water retentive materials (coir/peat) to 3 parts to 1 part drainage (coarse sand/perlite).

EXPECTATIONS

Haworthia don't tend to stretch as quickly as echeveria and many other succulents, so you won't need to propagate by top cutting as frequently. The formation of pups creates a compact clump that looks nice enough to keep intact for several years. Alternatively, you may opt to separate the pups to create more plants for yourself or to give to friends. Interestingly, haworthia tend to grow more during the cooler winter months and slow down in the heat of the summer. In some cases, the roots will die off in the summer but, as the temperature becomes cooler, the plant will reestablish roots.

TOP LEFT: I created this mixed haworthiopsis planter mostly for convenience, so I could water all of them at the same time.

TOP RIGHT: Various succulents basking under a grow light.

BOTTOM LEFT: Pups are forming at the base of this *Haworthiopsis coarctata*.

Haworthia Varieties to Collect

ABOVE LEFT: *Haworthiopsis limifolia*—commonly referred to as fairy's washboard.

TOP RIGHT: *Haworthiopsis resendiana* is a great long-term plant, as it can be propagated from cuttings once it gets too tall.

LEFT: From my mixed haworthiopsis planter: *H. glabrata* (left) and *H. attenuata* var. *radula* (right), with subtle differences in leaf texture.

OPPOSITE TOP LEFT: *Haworthiopsis attenuata* var. *radula* (left) and *H. attenuata* (back and right): it's fun to temporarily plant the pups into miniature pottery, but they should eventually be potted up to appropriately sized pots.

OPPOSITE MIDDLE LEFT: All of these may be casually referred to as cathedral window haworthia, but there are many different varieties shown here—various hybrids and cultivars of *Haworthia cooperi* and *H. obtusa*.

OPPOSITE BOTTOM LEFT: *Haworthia bayeri* (left) and *H. truncata* (right) with an emergent inflorescence.

OPPOSITE TOP RIGHT: *Haworthiopsis limifolia variegata*—a variegated and more expensive version of *H. limifolia*.

OPPOSITE BOTTOM RIGHT: *Haworthia maughanii* 'Rainbow' has flattened leaf tips.

In their natural habitat, hoyas can be found climbing up trees or trailing along the forest floor. The *Hoya* genus contains more than five hundred species and most have thick, stiff leaves with a dull appearance, which is well-suited to their common name: waxplant.

However, since many do have diverse foliage, not to mention extraordinary flowers, hoyas can become an addictive and expensive hobby, with so many species and hybrids to collect. Thankfully, hoyas propagate relatively easily, although a bit slower compared to some aroids—all you need is a stem cutting with a node to get started. If you begin a collection with mostly single-node cuttings, you can keep many hoya species in a relatively small space.

OPPOSITE: The *Hoya carnosa* 'Wilbur Graves' has extra splashy leaves compared to the regular *H. carnosa*.

Hoya growth expectations

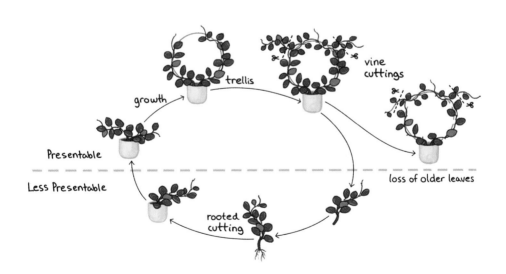

Presentable

Less Presentable

growth   trellis   vine cuttings

loss of older leaves

rooted cutting

ENVIRONMENT

Natural light: Three to four hours of direct sun is the upper limit, as long as you keep up with watering. For the rest of the day, indirect light at 200 FC (40 µmol) is sufficient, but better growth will occur above 400 FC (80 µmol).

Grow light: Aim for a DLI range of 4-10 mol/day; 8.6 mol/day can be achieved with 1000 FC (200 µmol) for 12 hours. Slightly slower development will occur at lower light levels, such as 600 FC (120 µmol) for 12 hours, which is 5.2 mol/day.

Nursery light: Hoyas are produced with light levels of 1500 to 2000 FC (approximately 80 percent shade).

Flowering occurs with good light—nursery conditions and grow-light usage can easily achieve this once the plant has reached maturity. For indoors, giving the plant the upper limit of direct sun will encourage flowering.

Temperature and Humidity: Hoyas will grow in temperatures of 18-29 C (65-85 F) and average room humidity (40-60 percent).

EFFORT

Watering: Hoya are quite tolerant of a completely dry substrate but will grow better if the dryness is not prolonged to the point of seeing wilting—leaves having a wrinkled appearance. Water when the substrate is about halfway dry.

Fertilizing: A fertilizer with NPK ratio 3-1-2 will work.

Substrate: Hoya are adaptable to both sphagnum moss-based substrates and peat/coir-based substrates. You can use a mixture of half sphagnum moss and half coarse bark chips or a standard potting soil (2 to 3 parts) with some added perlite or bark chips (1 part). Use more drainage material if light levels are expected to be on the lower side.

EXPECTATIONS

Hoyas will grow long vines that are suitable for hanging or wrapping up on a trellis. These vines can be easily damaged if the plant is frequently handled. As the vines begin to outgrow their support, you can take cuttings to keep the main plant looking tidy. The cuttings can be rooted in water or sphagnum moss and transplanted into a small pot—for example: 3 or 4 vines to a 4-inch pot. These make great gifts or, if your main plant is looking sparse, you can transplant them into your existing pot.

Hoyas flower on stalks called peduncles. These tend to look like bits of stem that have lost their leaves. When you see a structure like this on a hoya, be careful not to cut it off if you want your plant to flower.

Hoya Varieties to Collect

ABOVE: *Hoya compacta variegata*—the twisted/folded leaves remind me of fortune cookies. Kay provided adequate light for this mature specimen to produce several blooms.

OPPOSITE TOP LEFT: Genna's *Hoya latifolia* 'Sarawak' is blushing due to sun stress, which is a completely normal response from certain plants that can activate anthocyanin, a pigment that protects the plant from UV rays.

OPPOSITE TOP RIGHT: These two *Hoya linearis* hanging baskets get prime window locations.

OPPOSITE BOTTOM LEFT AND RIGHT: *Hoya caudata* leaves have a rough texture once matured (left) but start off soft and fuzzy (right).

Living with *Hoya mathilde*

Plant people are always looking at objects and thinking "Hey, I could plant something in this!" That was the thought I had when shopping for kitchen accessories and finding this sink sponge holder. The suction cups meant that it could be mounted to a window—the best place for plants! The *Hoya mathilde*'s small leaves made it an ideal candidate for such a planting.

Sphagnum moss is an ideal planting medium for this situation: With more surface area of the substrate exposed to air, I needed something that would hold water well and also not crumble apart, since this was not a traditional container.

The first step in the standard repotting procedure: loosen the old root-ball. The nursery was already using sphagnum moss, so I didn't feel the need to remove much of the current material.

Next, I lined the sponge holder with a layer of sphagnum moss.

This planting came to be known as the Hoya Taco!

1 year

Being mounted against the window meant the plant got the maximum possible view of the sky for excellent light. Along one of the new tendrils, I spotted the first peduncle—my *Hoya mathilde* will flower!

1 year, 8 months

Friends warned me that it would still be months before I would see any flower buds and there was the possibility of bud blast—when the buds develop but suddenly abort and fall off. This can happen if the plant experiences severe drought. This bud will make it!

At watering time, the planter felt right at home in the sink! Sphagnum moss tends to be more water retentive than traditional soil, which is why it worked well in this planting, where the plant was more exposed to air than in a typical pot. Whenever the moss was almost completely dry, I would take it to the sink for watering. First, I would moisten with plain tap water then water with 3-1-2 fertilizer dissolved into a watering can.

2 years

My *H. mathilde* has rewarded me with a lovely clump of blooms! All hoya flowers bloom in a globular formation with varying colors. The scent can be pungent with notes of vanilla, chocolate, and honey, but the nectar can be quite sticky!

3 years

As with any creative planting, there will come a time when the plant outgrows the planter or the care becomes burdensome. In this case, the small volume of sphagnum moss began to dry up sooner, making my job of watering an annoyingly frequent task.

Andrew created this adorable costume for his daughter, Gracie, which became the inspiration for the next phase of my *Hoya mathilde*: a circular trellis! Andrew happens to sell these exact trellises so I bought myself a few!

4 Years

I potted the *Hoya mathilde* into a plastic nursery pot with sphagnum moss and used a white cachepot similar to Gracie's costume. The vines were secured with short pieces of soft wire ties, which can be easily adjusted as the vines grow.

5 years

Setting the plant right in front of my southeast window gave it 2 or 3 hours of direct sun and indirect light in the 400–600 FC range, which yielded excellent growth. The vines pushed out many leaves, nicely filling in the trellis.

A Tale of Two Hoyas

Hoya kerrii is a popular Valentine's Day gift on account of its heart-shaped leaves. Unfortunately, many of these novelty items never grow into full plants because they are "blind cuttings"—a leaf cutting that can root but does not contain stem tissue, so a new growth point will never emerge. When I found a whole plant, I quickly bought it. As a bonus, the variety was variegated. Around the same time, I decided to dip my toes into the *Hoya* genus: *Hoya kerrii variegata* (bottom), *H. carnosa* 'Chelsea' (top left), and *H. carnosa* 'Krimson Princess' (top right). Let's follow two of them.

The thick leaves give the plant a succulent-like quality, so they can be planted in a well-draining potting soil and watered whenever the soil is completely dry. Unfortunately, relative to other hoyas, *H. kerrii* tends to be a bit slower to grow if your light levels are always indirect—in the 100–400 FC range. My plant remained generally the same size for about half a year.

The first sign of new growth! You can see this plant was cut so the new leaf emerged from the previous node.

8 months

As expected, the leaves grown in indirect light (100–400 FC) without any direct sun would not be as flat or variegated as those grown at the nursery (likely 1,000–5,000 FC most of the day).

1 year, 6 months

In my new apartment, the light situation was a bit better with 2 to 3 hours of afternoon sun and morning indirect light at 100–200 FC. The plant is starting to look a bit bigger than when first purchased!

3 years

I recently repotted the *H. kerrii* and put her into my Ikea greenhouse cabinet. The new growth seemed to explode as if it had been waiting for better light and a fresh pot of soil.

She got the prime real estate—top row, receiving 1,000 FC (180 µmol) of light for 12 hours a day (comes to a DLI of 7.8 mol/day).

4 years

Although the plant had lost a few leaves over the years, seeing this one retire was a bit harder because it was always a focal point (yes, it's okay to have favorite leaves!). Look back through the older photos—it's the one grabbing your attention!

Meanwhile, the 'Krimson Princess' looked great in its 6-inch pot, but I would later discover, when repotting, that there were root mealybugs. Root pests are a pain to deal with, so I decided to simply cut off a few of the vines for propagating.

1 year

Sometimes I treat propagation as a kind of horticultural horcrux—a means of extending the life of a plant by keeping some piece of it alive, even if the rest is gone.

1 Year, 6 Months

One should normally not leave a propagation in water for so long, but sometimes I procrastinate with potting up my propagations.

1 year, 9 months

I have finally gotten around to potting up the plant. Many people worry that if you leave a plant in water for too long, it won't do well in soil. Rest assured, if you provide the plant adequate light, its chances of survival are a lot better than you might think.

New light situation

On the top row of the greenhouse cabinet hanging out with other Hoya friends—*H. kerrii* and *H. mathilde*. Light data: receiving 1,000 FC (180 μmol) of light for 12 hours a day (equivalent to DLI of 7.8 mol/day).

1 month after entering the cabinet

New growth! I was overjoyed to see the bright blush of pink on the newest leaves—the main feature of this hoya. Now that the plant is in soil, I resumed the usual watering strategy for this plant: watered with 3-1-2 fertilizer whenever the soil was partially to nearly completely dry.

4 months after entering the cabinet (OPPOSITE)

The single vine is now long enough to propagate again, but I have become quite fond of this plant growing as a single vine—you don't necessarily need to have a large, overflowing pot with multiple vines in order to enjoy the plant!

158

Monstera

Self-portrait with my *Monstera deliciosa* 'Thai Constellation'.

The *Monstera* genus is best known for the *Monstera deliciosa*—the plain green classic. In recent years, cultivars with variegated leaves and diverse leaf structures have become popular. And, at the time of writing, they are not cheap. Uncommon monsteras are among the more desirable house plants today, with large social media followings of their own!

Monstera growth
expectations

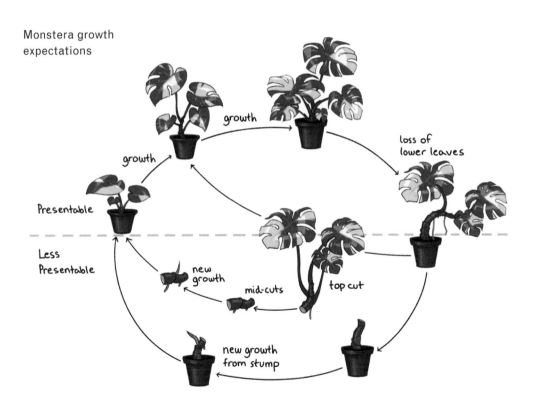

ENVIRONMENT

Natural light: For good growth, try to find a large-enough window to get indirect light close to 400 FC (80 μmol). Two to three hours of direct sun is tolerable for *Monstera deliciosa*, but you should be vigilant about checking the soil moisture. Direct sun should always be diffused for variegated cultivars.

Grow light: 400 FC (80 μmol) for 12 hours/day will provide a DLI of 3.5 mol/day, which should be sufficient.

Nursery light: Monsteras are commercially produced at 2,000–3,000 FC (70–80 percent shade).

Temperature and Humidity: Monstera will grow best in the temperature range of 18–29 C (65–85 F) and average room humidity (30–50 percent). The more delicate-leaved monsteras will do better with higher humidity (60–80 percent).

EFFORT

Watering: Water when the soil is partially dry. Observe the moisture content of your substrate—when it's about halfway between saturated and completely dry, then it's time to water. Monstera are drought tolerant, so they can recover from a dry spell, but their growth will be stunted.

Fertilizing: A fertilizer with NPK ratio 3-1-2 will work well for monstera. A liquid or slow-release fertilizer can be used.

Substrate: Standard potting soil (2 to 3 parts) with some added perlite or bark chips (1 part). Use more drainage material if light levels are expected to be on the lower side.

EXPECTATIONS

As a single vine planting, *M. deliciosa* will keep getting longer, continuously losing its lower leaves. There will come a point where the base is a long leafless stem. If you wish to maintain a neat, bushy plant, you can take the growing tip of the vine as a top cutting and root it in water, or just plant it directly into a suitable substrate. The remaining stem can be cut up and the pieces propagated as "wet-sticks" (that is, a piece of stem with at least one node) or, if the stem is left in the original pot, new growth points should emerge. Most collectors with the rarer cultivars will sell the lower parts of the stem and keep the growing tip, as this will have the highest degree of fenestration (see below) and should continue putting up similarly fenestrated leaves.

Occasionally, pups may form at the soil level. These can be removed to start another plant.

How do I get bigger leaves with the holes?

After 2 months, the plant receiving 19 mol/day (right) not only grew more leaves, but each leaf was progressively larger with side cuts. The plant receiving 0.3 mol/day (left) grew fewer and smaller leaves.

The holes and slits in a large monstera leaf are called fenestrations, from the French word *fenêtre*, meaning "window." The first few leaves from a new growth point (the juvenile leaves) start out as solid, heart-shapes, but with good growing conditions, subsequent leaves will develop more complexity.

The secret to developing more fenestrated leaves is in the amount of light the plant receives. I once ran a small-scale A/B test with two monstera pups from my larger plant, which means they were genetically identical to the mother plant.

Light situation 1: Under a strong grow light receiving about 1,900 FC (or 380 µmol) for 14 hours/day, which comes to a DLI of about 19 mol/day.

Light situation 2: Under indirect natural light measuring no higher than 50 FC (10 µmol) most of the day—if we assume this lasts 8 hours, the resulting DLI would be about 0.3 mol/day.

After 8 months, the newest leaves already have midrib holes. This plant is definitely ready for a bigger pot!

Variegation: Observations of *Monstera deliciosa* 'Thai Constellation'

Day 1

I wanted to try a variegated culti-var of *M. deliciosa*, so I got a small 'Thai Constellation', which is a mutation produced in a laboratory in Thailand. It features green leaves with white speckles that resemble a star-filled sky, although some leaves will have larger white patches. A small specimen is affordable for me, but the rate of growth is noticeably slower than the plain green monstera, so I'll need patience to wait for the fenestrated leaves to emerge.

1 year

The new leaves that have come out have fenestrations! Any monstera

owner would be overjoyed. With good growing conditions, the next leaves will have even more fenestrations. The light situation getting to this point was diffused sun measuring 1,000–2,000 FC (200–400 µmol) lasting roughly 3 hours with indirect light at 200–400 FC (40–80 µmol) the rest of the day. I watered with a 3-1-2 fertilizer whenever the soil reached 60–80 percent dry.

2 years

After a sizing up of the pot, we got hit with thrips. A few months of diligent physical removal and insecticidal soap spraying has kept the infestation under control, while leaving behind some battle scars on the lower leaves.

With the rapid leaf growth, it was time to repot again. As a rule of thumb with monsteras, you can size up the pot so that it is as large as the diameter of the largest leaf.

A young monstera's roots will grow aggressively, which means the plant will become root bound within a year. Be sure to loosen the root-ball prior to repotting—breaking a few roots here and there is OK, considering the majority will be free to explore new soil.

3 years (opposite)

The lowest leaf is turning yellow. That leaf happened to be the newest one on the plant at the end of our first year together. Consider that all the leaves from 2 years ago are now lost, but the overall plant still looks great, thanks to all the newer leaves that have emerged since then. After 4 years, my plant started getting some midrib fenestrated leaves (see page 160). The 'Thai Constellation' is definitely one of my favorites!

Variegation: Observations of *Monstera deliciosa* 'Albo Variegata'

Day 1 (top left)
Roos got a *Monstera deliciosa* 'Albo Variegata'. This cultivar offers more dramatic white variegation than 'Thai Constellation' and a subtly different growth pattern, but the main difference is that it's an unstable mutation, which means that the variegation may not appear on new leaves as they come in. If a stem reverts to solid green leaves, the only way to "bring back" variegation is to cut the reverted stem back to a stem section with variegation and wait for a new growth point. (You may find the same thing happens with some variegated pothos, but of course you won't have to wait as long for new leaves to come in!)

7 months (bottom left)
Roos decided to install a moss pole to support her monstera albo.

9 months (right)
When the main vine can take root against a vertical surface, the plant seems to grow much faster. Roos is ecstatic!

Supporting a Shingling *Monstera dubia*

Day 1

My new *Monstera dubia*! As with scindapsus, the juvenile leaves seem to seek out flat surfaces upon which they will grow like shingles—the technical term for this surface-growing is "appressed." Most growers can achieve good shingling with a rough wooden plank—the porous surface allows for good aerial root adhesion, which requires consistent moisture. While daily watering of a wood plank is easy in a nursery or outdoor setting, doing this indoors can become tedious.

4 months

I was able to keep the shingling action by creating a moss board. I lined a wooden board with sphagnum moss held in place with plastic mesh fencing. Some very modest grow lights (measuring just 200 FC for 12 hours a day, which works out to a DLI of 1.7 mol/day) helped the process along.

It takes time for the vine to root into the moss, so I used a small piece of rubber coated wire to secure it against the moss.

Monstera Varieties to Collect

ABOVE LEFT: *Monstera obliqua* 'Peru' has some of the most fenestrated leaves in the Monstera genus.

TOP RIGHT: Melissa's *Monstera deliciosa* 'Aurea'—similar to 'Thai Constellation' but with yellow/gold variegation. This is a stable mutation that will retain its variegation with good light.

BOTTOM RIGHT: *Monstera standleyana variegata*—its long shiny leaves resemble a pothos, but the variega-tion of white speckles with the occasional white sector is similar to the 'Thai Constellation.' The growth habit is vining, and several vines can be combined in a pot to create a nice planting. At lower light levels (DLI less than 2 mol/day or less than 200 FC most of the day), the internode spacing will be longer and leaves will progressively become smaller. If desired, these can be easily cut back and propagated as cuttings.

ABOVE LEFT: *Monstera karstenianum* is commonly known as Monstera Peru. The leaves have a bullate texture and are somewhat glossy. The vines can sometimes grow long, with diminishing leaf size, but you can always cut them up to propagate new plants. Train it onto a moss pole and the emergent leaves should be larger.

TOP RIGHT: *Monstera adansonii*—Dustin's plant had reached the top of the moss pole and started sending out long vines, or, as Dustin likes to call them, "green ropes." In the past, *M. adansonii* was sold as the more desirable *M. obliqua,* until a wave of social media aware-ness coined the phrase, "It's never obliqua!" With more photos showing the morphological differences between the two plants, collectors everywhere became better at identi-fying and distinguishing between the common *M. adansonii* and the rare *M. obliqua.*

BOTTOM RIGHT: Monstera 'Burle Marx's Flame' is an expensive hybrid. Dustin's plant has grown very well under a grow light with consistent thorough waterings and appropri-ate fertilizing. Notice the uppermost (newest) leaves have emerged with deep fenestrations, showing why this plant bears the name 'flame'.

Peperomia

The genus *Peperomia* comprises thousands of species, and many are fun to collect. They also don't tend to be too expensive, so you can grow a collection with a relatively modest budget. In terms of space, peperomias are generally small, cultivated in 4- to 8-inch pots, so they'll work well on a table, small shelf, or windowsill. And they have a range of growth habits—some grow on stems that keep getting taller while others stay compact, growing in a rosette form—and leaf shapes and colors, adding interest.

When the growing conditions are good and the plant has reached a certain age, all peperomias will send up a rat-tail-like inflorescence where the actual flowers are microscopic on the stalk. Some collectors suggest cutting them off so the plant focuses its growth resources to its leaves, but I like them.

OPPOSITE: Although peperomia leaves can be quite different, their flowers have a similar upright structure.

ENVIRONMENT

Natural light: You should get adequate growth if your average indirect light is above 100 FC (20 μmol), but the plant will do much better in the 400–800 FC range (80–160 μmol). Peperomia can tolerate an hour or two of direct sun. Use a white sheer curtain to diffuse the sun if the duration of direct exposure will be longer.

Grow light: Peperomia will do well with 200 FC (40 μmol) for 12 hours a day (equivalent to DLI 1.7 mol/day) but you can push it to grow more going up into the 400–800 FC range (80–160 μmol) for 12 hours a day (equivalent to DLI 3.5–6.9 mol/day).

Nursery light: Peperomia production in a greenhouse calls for 1,500–3,500 FC (300–700 μmol), which is around 70–90 percent shade.

Temperature and Humidity: Peperomia will grow well with daily temperatures in the 18–24 C (65–75 F) range. Most will grow well with average room humidity (40–60 percent).

EFFORT

Watering: Water a peperomia when its soil is just past halfway dry. Most peperomia are semi-succulent, having thick leaves, which makes them drought tolerant, but when the soil becomes completely dry, the plant will begin to wilt. Best to water before it reaches this point to avoid permanent root damage or plant tissue kinks. The softer stem varieties will droop as the soil reaches total dryness— when this happens, water immediately.

Fertilizing: A fertilizer with NPK ratio 3-1-2 will be suitable.

Substrate: Standard potting soil (2 to 3 parts) with some added perlite or bark chips (1 part). Use more drainage material if light levels are expected to be on the lower side.

EXPECTATIONS

Peperomia with a true stem will keep growing taller and eventually flop over. Take the top cutting at any time to reset the plant. Middle cuts can also initiate new growth points when laid on sphagnum moss or moist perlite in a propagation box. The remaining stump will also initiate a new growth point.

For rosette-type peperomias, such as *Peperomia argyreia* (watermelon peperomia) and any of the rippled leaved types, they too can be propagated by top cutting, but leaf cutting is the method preferred by commercial greenhouses. Cut a healthy leaf in half across its veins and insert it, cut side down, into any moist substrate. Ensure that the substrate never dries out—this is easier with an enclosed propagation box or humidity dome. Only modest light is required during propagation—try 100 FC (20 μmol) for 12 hours from a grow light or similar indirect light levels without any direct sun.

LEFT: Peperomia without a true stem, such as the watermelon peperomia seen here and any of the ripple leaf types, can be propagated by leaf cutting. New growth emerges from the veins of the old leaf.

Upright peperomia
growth expectations

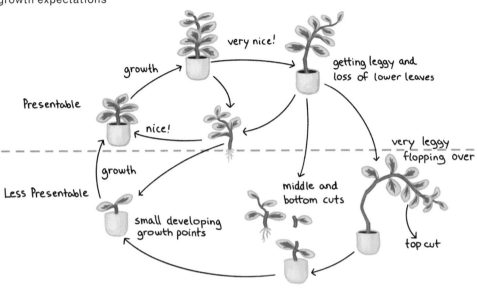

very nice!

growth

Presentable

nice!

getting leggy and
loss of lower leaves

very leggy
flopping over

growth

Less Presentable

small developing
growth points

middle and
bottom cuts

top cut

Rosette peperomia
growth expectations

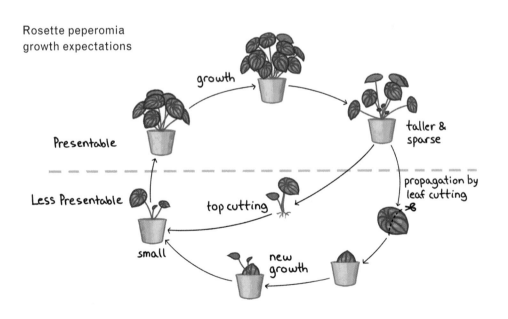

growth

Presentable

taller &
sparse

propagation by
leaf cutting

Less Presentable

top cutting

small

new
growth

Peperomia Varieties to Collect

ABOVE: A peperomia collection: *Peperomia obtusifolia* (left), *P. clusiifolia* (right), *P. prostrata* (back).

RIGHT: The watermelon peperomia, *Peperomia argyreia*, is eye-catching. When grown in a nursery where light is evenly diffused from all angles, the leaves arrange themselves in a lovely array. The plant does not grow from a true stem, but as a clump of petioles emerging from the soil.

Adopting a *Peperomia obtusifolia variegata*

Day 1

Looking for a fresh *Peperomia obtusifolia variegata* (also known as "baby rubber plant") to go to my wife's office to be her desk plant. We made sure there were adequately sized windows nearby.

1 year

The peperomia had to be transferred to me because my wife's office moved, and the new location was much darker as it was obstructed by tall buildings. I kept the plant in my office kitchen, which gave indirect light in the 200–400 FC range most of the day with occasional direct sun (no more than an hour due to outdoor obstructions). The peperomia still grew in a pleasing manner.

3 years

The leading stems were sticking out awkwardly, but I decided to let them keep growing to see what structure they would take on.

3 years, 6 months

Awkwardness is a matter of opinion. I think the gnarly stems exclaim "we belong here!" Plants are shaped by their light.

The Bonus *Peperomia puteolata*

Day 1

When I went to buy some plants from a nice woman, she added this bonus peperomia—a *Peperomia puteolata*! Commonly called parallel peperomia, *P. puteolata* has rigid leaves that grow in groups of threes or fours along a reddish stem. The spacing between nodes is strongly influenced by the daily average light levels, but the plant still looks nice with elongated stems, eventually forming a hanging growth habit. With 200 FC most of the day, the plant will grow well—better if you can also get an hour or two of direct sun.

1 month

The surest sign of a happy house plant—new leaves emerging!

1 year

Sitting in the kitchen windowsill at my office, the plant saw indirect light most of the day in the 200–400 FC range, with the occasional burst of direct sun never lasting more than an hour or so because of the taller buildings nearby.

2 years

Propagation of the *P. puteolata* can easily be done by taking stem cuttings and rooting them in water. If you leave enough stem below a leaf set, the stem will root in the water as the leaves naturally rest on the rim of your propagation vessel. I gave some propagations of the plant to two friends, Jesse and Jeannie. Jesse's plant is shown here. Giving away propagations can sometimes be a form of insurance—or for Harry Potter fans, a horticultural horcrux.

3 years

Devastation! My new apartment faces west, and because my unit was higher than most surrounding buildings, the sun would shine directly onto my plants for 3–4 hours a day. I left the peperomia behind some other plants, so I would occasionally forget to check on it for watering. Here's the thing with "bright indirect light" plants getting some direct sun: It's not that any direct sun will immediately kill the plant, it's that the water usage will be faster so your task of keeping up with watering is more difficult. The rapid water usage also means the plant may reach the critical wilting point sooner—as was the fate of my *P. puteolata*. Fortunately, my friend Jesse kept his plant growing enough to give me a new start! I put the cutting in a small vial of water, which rooted in a few weeks.

Caring for *Peperomia prostrata*

Day 1

Sometimes called string of turtles, the *Peperomia prostrata* is one of those plants that you could get lost in staring at all the tiny details. The disk-shaped leaves come in a variety of shapes and sizes: Some are plump, some have striking markings, and little tail-like flowers seem to spring up among the leaves.

1 year

A plant can occasionally spark your creativity in terms of making a special planter that compliments its form. I turned PVC piping into a 3-column planter for my *Peperomia prostrata* to accentuate its flowing nature.

1 year, 6 months

Spider mites! This is why it's important to isolate any pest-infested plants—insects can easily walk to nearby plants. I sprayed the plant with insecticidal soap, but I figured it would be a losing battle since the plant had far too many places to hide.

2 years

After months of consistent spraying, I decided to try resetting the plant by propagating as many healthy stems as possible. I laid the strands against some moist potting soil (a very shallow dish will do) and kept them in a propagation dome. Once they're rooted, I'll be able to restart the plant.

Philodendron

Philodendrons have always been a staple of the house-plant industry. Their large, glossy leaves (some velvety ones too) and clean growth habit have made them an all-time favorite collector plant genus. Some species and cultivars grow relatively quickly, which can be a blessing or a curse—you can bless your friends with cuttings within a short time (often within a year), but it may be challenging to keep up with a plant that keeps outgrowing your space! New philodendron species are being discovered all the time in tropical rainforests. And some old friends that used to be considered philodendrons have been reclassified to other genera in recent years. Like the plants themselves, the world of philodendrons is always changing.

OPPOSITE: Philodendrons and monsteras from Jan's collection—left to right, *Monstera siltepecana*, *M. dubia*, *Philodendron verrucosum*, and P. 'Glorious' (a cross between *P. gloriosum* and *P. melanochrysum*).

ENVIRONMENT

Natural light: If your average indirect light is in the 200–400 FC range (40–80 µmol), your philodendrons should grow nicely, which shouldn't be too difficult right in front of a large window. Direct sun for 1–2 hours is fine but any longer and you may find keeping up with watering difficult. Beyond that, you should use a white sheer curtain to diffuse the light.

Grow light: 400 FC (80 µmol) from a white LED grow light for 12 hours gets you 3.5 mol/day. In the lower range (1–2 mol/day), you may notice slower growth and longer internode spacing, which should not be an issue depending on the specific type of philodendron.

Nursery light: Commercially produced philodendrons are pushed to grow at 2,000–3,000 FC, which is about 70–80 percent shade.

Temperature and Humidity: Philodendron do well in the temperature range of 18–29 C (65–85 F) and average room humidity (30–50 percent). Many will do better with higher humidity (60–80 percent).

EFFORT

Watering: Philodendrons are forgiving of drought but do best when you can water them when halfway dry. Once the substrate dries further, there will be noticeable wilting. The plant will recover with a good thorough soaking. If you decide to use a chunky substrate in combination with good light, you could aim to keep the substrate evenly moist at all times—good light will drive good growth when supported by consistent soil moisture.

Fertilizing: Any fertilizer with NPK ratio 3-1-2 will work. When a plant requires frequent watering, consider using a slow-release fertilizer to save time.

Substrate: Standard potting soil (2 to 3 parts) with some added perlite or bark chips (1 part). If you have the time and energy for frequent watering, increase the ratio of the drainage material.

EXPECTATIONS

Philodendrons can be grown as trailing vines or climbing vines on a post or trellis. Either way, it's easy to keep the plant manageable by trimming the leading growth. And cuttings generally propagate easily.

Leaf Emergence Complications in Philodendron

Philodendrons occasionally produce deformed leaves. Collectors value their pristine leaves, and while I tend not to chase perfection, I still enjoy a perfect new leaf myself! The deformity occurs when the new leaf begins to emerge, but because of the lengthening of the leaf petiole, the body of the leaf bulges out while the tip of the leaf blade remains trapped in its sheath. The image of Cinderella's slipper not fitting on the foot of a stepsister comes to mind.

If you lightly mist the emerging leaf on a regular basis, this may help the new leaf emerge undamaged. In mild cases, your leaf will have a slight kink that will become less noticeable as the leaf matures. In the worst case, the new petiole, or leaf stalk, may pierce the leaf blade, leaving a hole that will remain with that leaf forever. The likelihood of this kink developing during leaf emergence depends on the species of plant.

Through my observations of my own plants and casually surveying social media, *Philodendron melanochrysum* and P. 'Pink Princess' tend to be most prone to getting stuck. Assuming you have average room temperature and humidity (40–60 percent), my advice is to try some light misting to assist with leaf emergence. And don't despair, there is always the next leaf to enjoy!

LEFT: An emerging philodendron leaf is trapped!

RIGHT: You may notice sticky droplets on petioles and sometimes on the base of leaves. These are extrafloral nectaries, which the plant uses to attract ants that, in turn, defend the plant from plant-eating insects like caterpillars. The presence of these droplets does not necessarily indicate that the plant is under attack, but you should still monitor for pests on a regular basis.

Philodendron Varieties to Collect

ABOVE AND CENTER: Philodendron 'Malay Gold'—this hybrid is often sold under several names, including 'Lemon-Lime', 'Golden Goddess', and 'Ceylon Gold'. It grows well as a trailing basket. In my apartment, receiving indirect light at about 200 FC and 2 or 3 hours of direct sun in the afternoon, the vines put out leaves with reasonable spacing. After a year (right), the basket had 4 strong vines, which cascaded down the plant stand and eventually turned back upward.

ABOVE RIGHT: *Philodendron erubescens* 'Red Emerald'—this cultivar is usually sold with several vines affixed to a wooden post, creating a stunning floor plant. The caretaker at a nursery was kind enough to give me the top cutting, since it had grown past the top of the post.

OPPOSITE TOP: Jan's *Philodendron melanochrysum* is progressing nicely up the moss pole (left), which he keeps consistently moist. New leaves emerge with

orange-copper tones (center) and gradually darken to velvety green (right).

OPPOSITE BOTTOM: *Philodendron tortum.* A plant weakened from being shipped overseas (left) can recover and produce stunning foliage. Here's the same plant 1 year later (right). Note, the previously yellowed leaves did not turn green, they were simply removed once fully yellowed.

ABOVE LEFT: *Philodendron pedatum*—the juvenile leaves are already nice to look at, but if you support the main vine with moisture, the mature leaves are even more magnificent!

ABOVE RIGHT: Cyril's *P. pedatum* var. *quercifolium* is a top cut from a mature plant.

OPPOSITE TOP LEFT: Philodendron 'Florida Ghost' is a hybrid of *P. pedatum* and *P. squamiferum*. On

Genna's plant, the newest leaves have a pale minty color that gradually becomes darker green as the leaf ages.

OPPOSITE TOP RIGHT: The Philodendron 'Florida Beauty' is also a hybrid of *P. pedatum* and *P. squamiferum*, but with cream and green variegation. Grace's plant is particularly striking!

OPPOSITE BOTTOM ROW: *Philodendron spiritus sancti*—this is one

of the most sought-after philodendrons, due to its rarity in cultivation and fascinating leaf structure. My plant (left) is still small. Dustin pushed his plant (right) with higher light (around 3,000 FC for 12 hours a day) and consistent watering/fertilizing—the results are amazing! Each new leaf grew to a larger mature state. It also helped to keep moist sphagnum moss around the stem as it got taller.

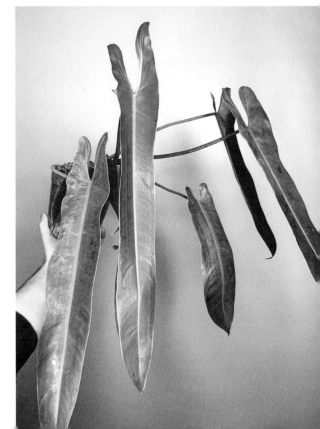

Platycerium

Is it a staghorn fern or an elkhorn fern? It actually doesn't matter, because these are common names and can refer to any number of platycerium plants, depending on who you ask. More importantly, when you begin collecting platyceriums, you are better off naming them according to their species names for clarity's sake. They are all fascinating plants to watch grow, especially when mounted to a board. Hang several, and you'll have a gallery of green trophies—except they are living!

OPPOSITE: Elliot's green trophies—an assortment of mounted ferns!

ENVIRONMENT

Natural light: You should get adequate growth if your average indirect light is above 200 FC (40 µmol), but the plant will do much better in the 400–800 FC range (80–160 µmol). Most platyceriums can tolerate 2–3 hours of direct sun, but it is critical to keep up with watering. Use a white sheer curtain to diffuse the sun if the duration of direct exposure will be longer.

Grow light: Ferns should receive at least 400 FC (80 µmol) for 12 hours/day for good growth (equivalent to DLI 3.5 mol/day).

Nursery light: 80 percent shade is used to produce most ferns, which translates to around 2,000 FC most of the day.

Temperature and Humidity: Platycerium will grow well with daily temperatures in the 16–32 C (60–90 F) range. Most will grow well with average room humidity (40–60 percent), but your task of keeping up with watering will be slightly easier with higher humidity (60–80 percent).

EFFORT

Watering: Most platyceriums are surprisingly drought tolerant, which is convenient when they're mounted—the substrate is more exposed to air and tends to dry out faster. Give your plant a thorough watering when the substrate is nearly completely dry.

Fertilizing: A high nitrogen fertilizer such as 3-1-2 diluted to half strength while the plant is actively growing will work well. Some growers suggest putting banana peels into the shield frond as a fertilizer, but this is only effective if the plant is growing in a natural environment, complete with the insect/animal life needed to consume the debris and excrete nutrients in a usable form for the plant. This will not work indoors unless there's also a colony of insects in your home!

Substrate: When grown in pots, a standard potting soil (3 to 4 parts) with some added perlite or bark chips (1 part) will do. When mounted, the ideal substrate is high-quality sphagnum moss, because it does not crumble apart. If you need some porosity, you can add some bark chips to the sphagnum moss.

EXPECTATIONS

A mounted platycerium may outgrow its mounting board after about a year of good growth. New shield fronds will continually cover the previous ones as new fertile fronds grow and older ones die. Keep an eye on the base of the plant for signs of new pups emerging. If your board is large enough, you can simply allow the new pups to keep growing, so the overall plant becomes more of a colony of platycerium plants. You can also separate the pups. You'll find it easier to start them in small pots until they are large enough to be mounted.

BELOW: With great growing conditions, platycerium can form a hanging colony. Here's a massive group growing at the New York Botanical Garden.

Platycerium Varieties to Collect

ABOVE: After much success and fond memories with my first platycerium—the standard "staghorn fern," *Platycerium bifurcatum*, which has the most antler-like fertile fronds (left)—I feel it would be a disservice to the plant collector to exclude it from this book. And here it is, 5 years later (right). From afar, this plant has grown well, but it had a bout with mealybugs—a year-long battle of constant removal and, as a last resort, a cold treatment. This only worked because the plant's tolerance of cold temperatures was lower than the mealybugs'.

The habit of *Platycerium bifurcatum* is to grow a basal or shield frond that wraps around the base of the plant and helps to keep the plant attached to the surface upon which it is growing (tree, board, or pot). The basal frond is referred to as the sterile frond because it does not develop spores for plant propagation. When the basal frond first begins to grow, it's a bright green color. Avoid touching or letting things bump into it, as the bruising will be permanent. Over a few months, it will slowly change to a brown color, and a new basal frond will grow on top of the old, brown one. After several years of growth, there will be multiple layers of old shield fronds beneath the surface.

The "antlers" are referred to as the fertile fronds, because when the plant reaches maturity, these fronds develop a dark brown patch on the undersides of the fronds—these are the spores. They can be harvested and sprouted to grow into more plants, but this can take several years, even in ideal conditions.

ABOVE: Benson's collection of freshly watered platycerium. Top: *Platycerium willinckii* 'Mt Lewis'; middle: *P.* 'Omo', *P. stemaria, P. ridleyi*; bottom: *P. hillii* 'Mio', *P. coronarium*.

RIGHT: Here's an impressive *Platycerium superbum* from Elliot's collection. His high-rise apartment with mostly unobstructed floor-to-ceiling windows is flooded with lots of light.

Growing *Platycerium wandae*

Day 1

A baby *Platycerium wandae*.

4 months

The *P. wandae* was definitely outgrowing its tiny pot, so I moved it to this old coffeepot lined with sphagnum moss. No drainage holes, no problem: Sphagnum moss doesn't crumble so I can easily pour out excess water from the spout.

1 year

The *P. wandae* doesn't have separate shield and antler fronds—instead, they grow together as one piece. This plant is ready to be mounted on a board! I described my technique for mounting staghorn ferns on boards in *The New Plant Parent*.

Rhaphidophora

Rhaphidophora tetrasperma is a climbing vine that develops similar fenestrations to monstera as it grows. Its small size compared to *Monstera deliciosa* gave this "mini monstera" a kind of cachet, and in the early days of collecting "rare" plants, *R. tetrasperma* was rather expensive—people were even buying leafless nodes in the hopes of growing a full plant. Thankfully for the rest of us, the plant grows rapidly and could easily be produced at scale. And since then, other interesting species in the *Rhaphidophora* genus have become available, including several with a shingling growth habit.

OPPOSITE: *Rhaphidophora decursiva* (center) develops talon-like leaves. *R. tetrasperma* (bottom) is sometimes called mini monstera.

ENVIRONMENT

Natural light: You can get good growth with low light—a mere 100 FC (20 µmol) most of the day without any direct sun will still lead to leaf production, but internodal spacing will be long, maybe 3 or 4 inches apart. Better growth and fenestrations will occur at indirect light levels in the 400–800 FC range (80–160 µmol). Direct sun tolerance is about 2–3 hours if you can keep up with watering.

Grow light: Set your rhaphidophora under a grow light to receive around 80 µmol (400 FC) for 12 hours—it should grow very well. The DLI will be 3.5 mol/day.

Nursery light: Commercial production of rhaphidophora calls for 70–80 percent shade, which measures 1,500–3,000 FC.

Temperature and Humidity: Rhaphidophora will grow well in the 21–35 C (70–95 F) range. Most will grow well with average room humidity (40–60 percent), but some prefer a little higher (60–80 percent) to maintain very nice leaves.

EFFORT

Watering: Water a rhaphidophora when partially dry. Wilting will occur as the soil approaches total dryness—you should avoid waiting until this point to water, although the plant should recover.

Fertilizing: A fertilizer with NPK ratio 3-1-2 will be suitable.

Substrate: Standard potting soil (3 to 4 parts) with some added perlite or bark chips (1 part). Use more drainage material if light levels are expected to be on the lower side.

EXPECTATIONS

Rhaphidophora tetrasperma shows its fenestration even without being rooted against a moss pole. If you want a monstera-like plant and you don't have a lot of space, this is a good choice.

Supporting *Rhaphidophora tetrasperma*

Day 1

Jon's freshly potted *R. tetrasperma*. The plant is set up for success in a nursery pot and outer ceramic cachepot. Jon has exceptionally large west-facing windows, so the plant gets great light even at a distance. From this position, the plant saw about 2 or 3 hours of direct sun and indirect light in the 400–800 FC range the rest of the day.

2 months

This fast grower needs something to climb or else the leading growth will produce subsequently smaller leaves—or no leaves at all. Here's *R. tetrasperma* on a moss pole.

4 months

Because it weighs less than a monstera, you can also grow *R. tetrasperma* on a small trellis, or even a strong branch, as here. Once the plant has surpassed its vertical support, you can cut off the leading growth, root it in water or a propagation box, and transplant it with the original plant, creating a fuller overall planting.

Rhaphidophora Varieties to Collect

OPPOSITE AND LEFT: *Rhaphidophora cryptantha*—a starter plant (opposite) sends out a new vine. Make sure you get it onto a vertical support as soon as possible so it can shingle its way up. Left, here's how the *R. cryptantha* grows along an upright surface. This plant belongs to my friend James in Singapore, where it can grow outside on his balcony.

TOP LEFT: *Rhaphidophora hayi*—commonly cultivated on a wooden board to support its shingling growth habit.

TOP RIGHT: *Rhaphidophora decursiva*—each new leaf will have a unique fenestration pattern.

Scindapsus

For a long time, *Scindapsus pictus*, commonly referred to as satin pothos (but unrelated to epipremnum) has been widely available and sold as a hanging basket. Indeed, its leaves have a satin finish with lovely silver flecks. As house-plant enthusiasts dove deeper into collecting, they found more species in the *Scindapsus* genus to acquire, grow, and love.

OPPOSITE: A lovely collection of scindapsus deserves its own set of shelves!

ENVIRONMENT

Natural light: You should get adequate growth if your average indirect light is above 100 FC (20 µmol), but the plant will do much better in the 400–800 FC range (80–160 µmol). Scindapsus can tolerate an hour or two of direct sun, but watch for the leaf curling, which should signal you to water immediately. Use a white sheer curtain to diffuse the sun if the duration of direct exposure will be longer.

Grow light: Scindapsus will do well with 200 FC (40 µmol) for 12 hours a day (equivalent to DLI 1.7 mol/ day), but you can push it to grow more in the 400–800 FC range (80–160 µmol) for 12 hours a day (equivalent to DLI 3.5-6.9 mol/day).

Nursery light: Scindapsus production in a greenhouse calls for 1,500–3,500 FC (300–700 µmol), which is around 70–90 percent shade.

Temperature and Humidity: Scindapsus will grow in temperatures of 18–29 C (65–85 F) and average room humidity (40–60 percent). Shingling plants will grow better with higher humidity.

EFFORT

Watering: Scindapsus can tolerate totally dry soil as its leaves store some water, but they will curl downwards if the plant is left dry for too long. Resist the temptation to use leaf curling as the easy sign to water and instead observe the soil— when it's roughly halfway dry, that should be your cue to water. If you are growing the plant on a vertical surface for shingling, you will need to keep the moisture high to encourage rooting.

Fertilizing: A fertilizer with NPK ratio 3-1-2—either liquid or slow-release will work.

Substrate: Standard potting soil (3 to 4 parts) with some added perlite or bark chips (1 part). Use more drainage material if light levels are expected to be on the lower side.

EXPECTATIONS

When the vines of a scindapsus flow freely down from the pot, they tend to gradually produce smaller leaves and maybe even some leafless nodes. Eventually, the plant will appear to be more vine than leaves. Thankfully, these plants propagate easily as node cuttings—even pieces of stems without leaves will propagate! You can root cuttings in water or simply lay a bunch of nodes onto a bed of moist sphagnum moss in a sealed container. When the cuttings begin to root and send out new shoots, you can pot them up together.

ABOVE: "Scindapsus Salad"— propagating various types of scindapsus together in an upcycled mixed greens box.

LEFT: If a scindapsus vine finds its way onto a flat surface, it can root against the surface and the subsequent leaves will grow appressed on the surface—this growth habit is called shingling.

Scindapsus Varieties to Collect

TOP LEFT: *Scindapsus pictus* 'Exotica'—pronounced silver patches and, on average, larger leaves than most scindapsus.

TOP RIGHT: *Scindapsus* 'Tricolor Borneo' (left) and *Scindapsus* 'Snake Skin' (back right) being propagated at a nursery.

LEFT: Scindapsus 'Silver Hero'.

TOP LEFT: *Scindapsus treubii* 'Moonlight' with silvery leaves.

TOP RIGHT: *Scindapsus pictus* 'Silver Lady' (left) and *S. pictus* 'Argyraeus' (right).

RIGHT: *Scindapsus treubii* 'Dark Form' has glossy dark-green foliage, unlike the "satin" feel of most other scindapsus.

Reviving *Scindapsus pictus* 'Argyraeus'

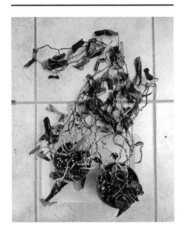

Here's the *Scindapsus pictus* 'Argyraeus' from my first book, *The New Plant Parent,* not looking so great. If your space is too crowded with plants, some may become difficult to reach and may be overlooked for watering. If this situation persists, the root system may suffer from permanent wilt.

Not to worry. Scindapsus propagates very easily by stem cuttings. I took the healthiest leaves and put their nodes into water. New roots were visible on the cuttings in water after a month, so they were transplanted into soil.

During the recovery, I wanted to make sure the light was strong enough to produce high-quality leaves. On this shelf, the plant was exposed to a grow light and receiving about 600 FC (120 µmol).

4 months

I was very pleased with this new leaf! With some patience, you can usually reset any plant and enjoy it all over again.

8 months

Strong light encourages shorter internode spacing and more striking foliage patterns.

Syngonium

Popular as a hanging basket, *Syngonium podophyllum* has long been known as arrowhead vine. Collectors enjoy the range of leaf patterns and colors that can be found in the many varieties of syngonium. It's common to find leaves with splashes of pink, yellow, white, cream, and pastel green— and since this kind of variegation is random, each new leaf is highly anticipated. Juvenile leaves are typically shield-shaped, but after a few new leaves, syngoniums develop more complex leaves, usually having two lobes, and some may have more.

OPPOSITE: A diverse collection of smaller syngonium varieties.

ENVIRONMENT

Natural light: If you don't mind slightly longer internode spacing, syngonium can grow with indirect light in the 100–200 FC range (20–40 µmol) but will do better with 400–800 FC (80–160 µmol). Duration of direct sun should not exceed an hour or two, as the leaves tend to fade and dry up.

Grow light: When you set your grow light so your syngonium receives around 400 FC (80 µmol) for 12 hours, it should grow very well. The DLI will be 3.5 mol/day.

Nursery light: Syngonium are commercially produced with 70–80 percent shade, which measures 1,500–3,000 FC.

Temperature and Humidity: Syngonium will grow well with daily temperatures in the 21–35 C (70–95 F) range. Most will grow well with average room humidity (40–60 percent) but some prefer a little higher (60–80 percent) to maintain very nice leaves.

EFFORT

Watering: Syngonium will do best if watered when partially dry. Wilting will occur as the soil approaches total dryness—you should avoid waiting until this point to water, although the plant should recover.

Fertilizing: A fertilizer with NPK ratio 3-1-2 will be suitable.

Substrate: Standard potting soil (3 to 4 parts) with some added perlite or bark chips (1 part). Use more drainage material if light levels are expected to be on the lower side.

EXPECTATIONS

Larger baskets of syngonium are sold when their foliage creates a nice bushy shape, but after a few months of growth, their vines will reach far beyond the pot. If you want to keep a more compact appearance, trim the plant back and propagate these cuttings. Root them in water or moist sphagnum moss. Even leafless nodes, if healthy, will sprout new growth. A heat mat will help with the rooting process. You can also grow syngonium on a pole if you want a vertical plant.

RIGHT: Arrowhead vine (*Syngonium podophyllum*) is a classic house plant.

Syngonium Varieties to Collect

TOP LEFT: *Syngonium wendlandii* features dark green foliage with a contrasting central stripe.

TOP MIDDLE: The *Syngonium mojito*'s variegation is reminiscent of the marble queen pothos.

TOP RIGHT: *Syngonium podophyllum* 'Pink Splash'—it's always exciting to see how splashy the next leaf will be as the pink flecks are random mutations.

BOTTOM LEFT: The *Syngonium podophyllum* 'Pink Perfection' has bright pink emergent leaves that gradually fade to a mixture of green and pink. This leaf is quite close to my skin tone!

BOTTOM MIDDLE: Syngonium T24— the newest leaves are pale with bright pink veining and eventually develop deeper green.

Thaumatophyllum

Popular house plants in the genus Thaumatophyllum, with their distinctive split leaves, used to be commonly referred to as philodendrons, but something about their stems always struck me as being different. Whenever an older leaf retires from the base of the growing tip, it leaves behind a prominent eye-like marking. As the plant keeps growing, the trunk clearly commemorates the leaves that have passed on. You don't see that in philodendrons.

To make matters more confusing, *Thaumatophyllum bipinnatifidum* was once thought to be a different plant from *Philodendron selloum*, which was known as the split-leaf philodendron. Genetic research has shown that these are actually the same plant, assigned today to the genus Thaumatophyllum.

The observed differences in leaf shape are therefore a testament to how varied leaf morphology can be determined by a plant's environment and age.

OPPOSITE: The trunk of a mature thaumatophyllum remembers the leaves the plant has lost.

ABOVE: When grown as a landscape plant (left), the *Thaumatophyllum bipinnatifidum* forms a large bush. It can thrive even if somewhat rootbound (right).

ENVIRONMENT

Natural light: Thaumato-phyllum can handle a lot of light, so, when indoors, the more the better—aim for 400–800 FC (80–160 µmol) indirect light and up to 4–5 hours of direct sun (if your windows are large enough). The plant will tolerate down to 200 FC (40 µmol) for average indirect light.

Grow light: It might be difficult to light the large *T. bipinnatifidum* completely under a grow light, but you can aim for 400 FC (80 µmol) for 12 hours – this is a DLI of 3.5 mol/day.

Nursery light: Greenhouse light levels for thaumato-phyllum should be in the 3,000–5,000 FC (600–1,200 µmol) range.

Temperature and Humidity: Thaumatophyllum will grow well with daily tempera-tures in the 21–35 C (70–95 F) range. Average room humidity (40–60 percent) is fine.

EFFORT

Watering: Water when the soil is partially dry. The plant is forgiving, so you will not notice too much wilting when the soil is completely dry.

Fertilizing: A high-nitrogen fertilizer (3-1-2) will ensure the plant can support about a dozen active leaves at the growing tip.

Substrate: Standard pot-ting soil (2 to 3 parts) with some added perlite or bark chips (1 part). Use more drainage material if light levels are expected to be on the lower side.

EXPECTATIONS

When left growing for decades, a thaumatophyl-lum can continually put out new leaves at the growing tips of the plant and have a massive, winding trunk. Some botanical gardens have truly impressive specimens! Since you surely have less space than a botanical garden, when your thaumatophyllum grows well beyond the soil surface, restart the plant by air-lay-ering somewhere along the stem. Once roots form, you can plant your cutting in a new pot. The lower section can sprout new growth, but the first few leaves might be substantially smaller than the ones on the growing tip. In time, new leaves will get bigger. Thankfully, a thaumatophyllum's trunk is a desirable and distinctive feature, so you can enjoy it for many years before decid-ing if you want to restart the plant.

OPPOSITE AND RIGHT: *Thaumatophyllum xanadu*—you can think of this as a mini version of the *T. bipinnatifidum*. It has the same distinctive markings on its trunk, but the leaves are finger-like and smoother than the larger *T. bipinnatifidum*, which tend to be more ruffled. The distinctive trunk (opposite) is a perfect illustration of completely normal leaf turnover: Each marking on the trunk is the scar of a retired leaf. As long as the yellowing leaf is an older one (as in, the lowest along the trunk among the current set of leaves), you can calmly remove it—the plant is fine. Be sure to thank it for its contribution to photosynthesis!

LEFT: A mature *Thaumatophyllum spruceanum* produces a beautiful compound leaf (left). It has the familiar trunk shared by all thaumatophyllum (right).

Tillandsia

Tillandsia are great for collecting if you have a small space and would rather not deal with soil. They're called air plants because their natural habitat is to live perched on tree branches. Air plants sometimes appear to have silvery hair—these outgrowths are called trichomes. They help the plant absorb moisture by increasing the surface area exposed to the air. Different species of air plants have different trichome structures—some are hardly noticeable, giving the plant more of a smooth green color, while others are so pronounced that the plant looks furry.

ABOVE: My bathroom windowsill is filled with tillandsias.

ENVIRONMENT

Natural light: Ensure the indirect light range is 200–400 FC (40–80 µmol) most of the day, and 2–3 hours of direct sun would be helpful. Generally, if direct sun exposure will exceed 3 hours, then block it with a white sheer curtain. The degree of trichome coverage can give you a clue about that plant's tolerance for direct sun. The *Tillandsia tectorum*, having the most prominent trichomes, will grow well with 3 or 4 hours of direct sun when you keep up with watering.

Grow light: Set them at a distance that gives 400 FC and keep them on for 12 hours—this will be a DLI of 3.5 mol/day.

Nursery light: 3,000–5,000 FC (approximately 50–70 percent shade) will work well for tillandsia.

Temperature and Humidity: Tillandsia can be grown in a wide temperature range: 10–32 C (50–90 F) but will do best closer to the middle rather than the extremes. Average room humidity (40–60 percent) is fine for tillandsia.

EFFORT

Watering: Since tillandsia do not root themselves in a substrate, you need to be more regimented for watering—don't put your air plants in some fancy display and forget about them! Outdoors with good light, you can spray or soak your air plants in a pool of water approximately once a week. Shorten the time interval during hot spells. Indoors, soak the plants in a sink or a tub weekly for 20–30 minutes. It is a good idea to shake off excess water from the air plant after watering, so as to prevent crown rot.

Fertilizing: In terms of fertilizing, a dilute dose (perhaps a quarter the recommended strength) of liquid 3-1-2 fertilizer into their bathwater will be good. This can be done once a month during the growing season.

EXPECTATIONS

The life span of an individual air plant is a few years until it flowers. Once the flowers fade, that plant stops growing and begins to decay. If the plant had good growing conditions, it should have started producing a pup—a little baby version of the mother plant growing off the base. You can keep the pup attached to the mother plant indefinitely, creating a clump of air plants. Or you can remove the pup once it has grown to roughly two-thirds the size of the mother plant. Be careful not to remove the pup too soon as it may never fully develop into an adult plant!

ABOVE: My weekly air plant soaking tub.

TOP LEFT AND RIGHT: I accidently broke off the little pup from this *Tillandsia pruinosa* (left). Hoping it would still grow, I cared for it along with all my other air plants. After two years (right photo, bottom middle) the little runt never fully developed into the characteristic bulbous shape of a mature *T. pruinosa* (right photo, top left). As with all air plants after flowering, they stop growing and slowly fade away (right photo, top right).

LEFT: Watering a collection of tillandsia naturally in the rain!

Tillandsia Varieties to Collect

Tillandsia andreana—an orb-like structure with fine leaves. When the plant reaches maturity, it produces a brilliant red flower.

LEFT: *Tillandsia tectorum* reminds me of a fuzzy sea urchin that lives in trees. It has the most pronounced trichomes of all air plants. When wet (top left), the trichomes are pressed against the leaf, giving the plant an overall green appearance—almost looking like a round *T. ionantha*. Watch the plant over the next few hours to see how the trichomes bounce back up (bottom left), regaining the fuzzy appearance.

OPPOSITE TOP LEFT: The *Tillandsia xerographica* is often called the queen of air plants, on account of its majestic ribbon-like leaves. The structure of the plant makes it perfect for capturing water, but be sure to shake off the excess.

OPPOSITE TOP RIGHT: *Tillandsia ionantha* is the quintessential air plant that is often glued to a piece of driftwood or into a glass orb, creating a nice display. While this makes a nice gift, it's not the best for long-term maintenance of the plant. The species has many enticing cultivars. Here *T. ionantha* 'Peanut' (left), forming a clump after several years of growth, and *T. ionantha* 'Macho' (right).

LEFT: *Tillandsia ionantha* 'Evolution'—most air plants turn slightly red when they start to flower. The picture on the right was taken about a month after the one on the left.

Observations of *Tillandsia funckiana*

Although it resembles a clipping from a pine tree, the *Tillandsia funckiana* will continue growing just fine with regular watering and good light (200–400 FC most of the day should be sufficient, but an hour or two of direct sun would be great).

If you're not watering regularly enough, the older leaves will become dry and die. With some strategic pruning, however, the dead part can be clipped off, leaving the newest and hopefully healthy growth to continue.

The *T. funckiana* produces pups when growth conditions are good, so the goal is, in a few years, to have a little clump of plants that you can hang proudly in your window. And if you should happen to have a greenhouse, after fifty years, your plant might look like this!

The Life Cycle of *Tillandsia caput-medusae*

Day 1

Tillandsia caput-medusae—so named for its Medusa-like leaves that tend to curl up tightly when the plant is desperately dry. Here I've started a small collection of *T. caput-medusae* plants—the light situation was a short burst of direct sun for about 1 hour in the morning and the rest of the day, indirect light at around 400 FC. Having another house close to the window actually helped with diffusely reflecting the sun in the afternoon. Without the reflection, the indirect light levels would be closer to 100–200 FC. I was excited to find the specimen in the corner as it was abnormally large.

1 month

Both my smallest and largest specimens started producing flowers! *T. caput-medusae* comes in a wide range of sizes, mostly likely having to do with the way the plants are grown at the nursery.

1 year

One of them is now on its second pup while both sets of flowers have completed their blooming process. It is often stated that air plants die after they flower but that doesn't mean they will immediately disintegrate, it just means the plant no longer grows and gradually declines, as it lives on (genetically) through its pups.

4 years

After an air plant is freshly watered, its trichomes are closed and the plant's surface is moist, giving a deep green appearance. Most people cut off the spent flower stalks, but I decided to keep them as souvenirs—the third pup's flowers are on the way!

Appendix: Dealing with Pests

The reality of house-plant pests is this: Everyone will eventually have to deal with them! There's really no getting around pest infestations if you're frequently bringing home new plants. If you're not familiar with the various pests, then the infestation may become so severe that throwing away the entire plant is the best option to save the rest of your collection (and your sanity).

There are two key aspects of pest control that will help you win the war: pest detection and persistent treatments. Even experienced plant owners can miss the early signs of an infestation, as most pests lay eggs that are hidden somewhere on the plant or in the soil. That's why vigilance—constantly observing your plant collection for any sign of pest activity—is the best way to ensure that you lose the fewest plants to pests. If you're new to collecting plants, you may only notice an infestation by obvious leaf deformities or large formations of insects. In this section, my goal is to sharpen your eye for detecting the pests themselves, in the adult, larvae, and egg stages. If you're able to see pests early on, your chances of eradicating them will be better.

When you detect pest activity, isolate the affected plant from the rest of your collection—practice botanical social distancing. Keep the plant at least six feet away from other plants. If plants' leaves are touching, that's just an invitation! And most pests can crawl to nearby plants across hard surfaces.

Part of the difficulty in achieving complete eradication is that the treatments we use simply miss a small percentage of the pests. Therefore, persistent treatment is simply the reality of treating pests—they won't all die in one go. After each treatment, assume there are some eggs hidden on the plant—or, in the case of thrips, in the plant. The strategy is to keep treating until the reproductive cycle of the pest is broken.

Most people only notice scale when there are hundreds of little brown domes all along their leaves accompanied by sticky residue. The dome, an immobile protective shell that resists insecticidal soap sprays, is the last stage of the insect. Inside the dome are the eggs. When they hatch, the "crawlers" move along the plant and find a new place to settle and suck out the sugary fluids from the plant. If left unchecked, scale will completely overrun your plant, leaving you no choice but to discard it.

The crawlers are difficult to detect—they are small and hide in the nooks and crannies along the plant. Your first response should be to cut off heavily infested plant material. The amount you can (or are willing to) cut off depends on the plant: A pothos may have many leaves to spare but one leaf off your anthurium might be a quarter of its foliage. Weigh out the cost/benefit for yourself. If you're interested in keeping the plant long term, then cutting off infested foliage is a highly effective way to reduce the scale population. If your plant is still healthy, new leaves will grow.

After removal of plant material, your next action can be physical removal of the scale insects themselves. I have found masking tape and, for larger leaves, a lint roller, to be more effective than an alcohol dipped cotton swab (the usual suggested treatment). With the tape, you can be certain that the insect has been removed along with any crawlers nearby. Masking tape generally will not leave any residue and is less damaging than alcohol.

You can finish off your treatment with spraying insecticidal soap, which will hopefully kill off any crawlers that you weren't able to see. Every few days, as you inspect the plant, you can use the masking tape method to spot-kill any scale that you see while, on a weekly basis, do a more thorough insecticidal soap spraying.

The life cycle of scale from egg to adult is 30–60 days, with every adult capable of producing hundreds of crawlers, so repetition and consistent spot-killing are the keys to keeping the population under control. Expect to continue these treatments for a month or two.

ABOVE: Get to know the details of your plants so you can become better at identifying unwanted guests.

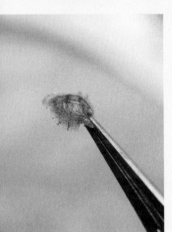

TOP ROW: A single adult scale—the protective dome may resemble a part of the plant, an aerial root nub perhaps.

BOTTOM LEFT AND CENTER: But it can be carefully removed to reveal a fortress of crawlers waiting to expand their operation.

BOTTOM RIGHT: Masking tape effectively pulls off the larger adult scale domes and any nearby crawlers.

The adult female mealybug is what most people can easily identify—an oval-shaped body with distinct antennae (although this is the rear of the insect). As they bite into the plant surface to suck out the juices, they also secrete a waxy protective layer in which to lay their eggs. In order to get the infestation under control, you should become familiar with the younger life stages of the mealybug—the nymphs are much smaller, oval-shaped, and without antennae. The males are winged and resemble a fungus gnat, but they don't fly as quickly. It's generally quite rare to see a male mealybug unless you have a severe infestation.

Cutting off heavily infested foliage is a sure way to decrease the mealybug population—this is an especially good option if your plant is due for a pruning anyway! A cotton swab dipped in alcohol is an effective way to spot-kill the larger adult females. You may need to use tweezers to get into the leaf sheaths where nests could be forming. Masking tape is a good way to pick up the nymphs, nests, and eggs.

Mealybugs tend to lay their eggs in nooks and crannies along the plant stem but, more deviously, on the outside and underneath the pot. So even if you think you've killed every mealybug on the plant, there could still be nests under the pot. These can be wiped off with an alcohol-dipped cotton swab or you can simply change the pot.

The life cycle of mealybugs from egg to adult is 60–90 days, with every adult capable of producing 300–600 eggs. Expect to continue monitoring for mealybugs and treating the plant for the next 2–3 months.

OPPOSITE: Fully grown mealybugs are easy to spot.

TOP ROW: Earlier stages of mealybugs can be harder to see—but now you know what to look for.

BOTTOM ROW: Why do mealybugs keep coming back? Because their hatcheries are hiding underneath the pot—and even under the lip of the pot!

As if regular mealybugs weren't scary enough, there is another kind of mealybug that attacks the roots of your plants. They are difficult to detect unless you make a point of checking for them—simply lift the plant out of its pot and inspect the roots. The ideal time to do this would be while repotting, but even in between waterings at the soil's driest point would be acceptable.

A plant infested by root mealybugs will have difficulty absorbing water since its root system is damaged. I once had a hoya that I was watering at the appropriate time, but the leaves just seemed to remain wrinkly and floppy after several months. It wasn't until I went to repot the plant that I discovered the root-ball was littered with white clumps.

With a mild infestation, you can try soaking the root-ball in a diluted solution of hydrogen peroxide. You can also try cutting out those infested sections with scissors and tweezers. With very severe infestations, if you wish to keep the plant, you can sever the entire plant from its root system and get the plant to create new roots by discarding the old root system. This is essentially propagating the entire plant as cuttings. It can be done!

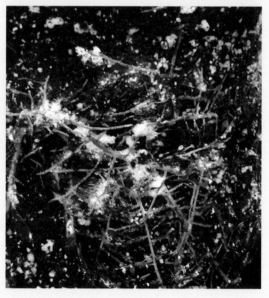

RIGHT: You may not discover root mealybugs until you repot the plant.

Fungus gnats are little flies that flutter around erratically and sometimes land in your coffee (which has happened to me). In comparison to the other pests listed here, fungus gnats are minimally damaging to plants, if exceptionally annoying to us humans. The larvae breed in the soil and feed on fungus in the soil. If you happen to disturb the soil surface, you might see some small, silvery crawling things, which are the fungus gnat larvae.

With the adults, you can purchase yellow sticky traps and put them in the soil. I have also used a small dish of fragrant dish soap, placed next to plants with fungus gnats. After a couple days, the adults have flown over and gotten stuck in the dish soap. If you happen to figure out which plants have fungus gnat larvae in the soil, you can water with a mix of Mosquito Bits. If the infestation is severe, repot the plant, replacing as much soil as possible.

ABOVE: Fungus gnats, in small numbers, are generally harmless to plants.

BELOW: A small bowl of dish soap easily attracts and captures adult fungus gnats, preventing them from laying more eggs in the soil.

There are several types of very small mites (smaller than 1 mm in length) that consume and destroy plant collections. If you notice what appears to be grains of sand that, when gently blown on, seem to be stuck to the leaf, you are likely dealing with spider mites. As an infestation gets worse, you may begin to see fine webbing and grainy damage on leaf surfaces. There is another type of spider mite that does not have visible webbing, so you may need to look for leftover eggshells or leaf damage indicators such as pin pricks or scratches. For certain plants like ficus, spider-mite damage causes some sap to oxidize with the air, leaving red markings that are easily visible.

In terms of dealing with spider mites, first, I see if I can cut off heavily infested foliage. Then I use a piece of tape to try to physically remove as many as possible. Then I spray with insecticidal soap and wipe down the leaves as much as I can, as spider mites lay their eggs on the leaf surface.

The life cycle of spider mites is 30–60 days from egg to adult. Every adult female lays about 100 eggs every 5–10 days. To break the reproductive cycle, you should treat the plant every 5 days over the next month or two.

ABOVE: Fine webbing between leaves is the sign of an already well-established infestation.

OPPOSITE: If you see the tiniest speck that does not fly away when you try to blow it off, go in for a closer look as it might be a spider mite or spider mite shells.

The adult thrips are small, slender, black or dark-brown insects, usually about 1 mm in length. Larvae are light yellowish and translucent, and even smaller than adults. They damage plants with their rasping mouthparts, which make silvery scratch marks on the leaves' surface. You may also see little black droplets—these are the excrement of thrips. What makes thrips the most difficult pests to eradicate is that they lay their eggs inside the plant tissue, so any wiping or spraying doesn't touch the eggs at all.

Your first line of defense should be to cut off heavily infested foliage. Look especially for damaged leaf areas, as this is likely where there are thrips' eggs implanted into the plant tissues. Removing these leaves is a worthwhile sacrifice.

Physically remove as many thrips as possible with a piece of masking tape. With a bigger leaf, you can use a lint roller. Follow up by spraying the entire plant with insecticidal soap. I like to keep some masking tape near the plant so if I happen to observe any thrips activity, I can use the tape for a spot treatment.

The thrips life cycle is 20–40 days from egg to adult. Each adult can lay 25–50 eggs, which hatch in about a week. Treating the plant every 5 days with continuous spot treating (masking tape) over the next 1–2 months is your best chance at breaking the reproductive cycle.

ABOVE AND OPPOSITE TOP ROW: Small patches of discoloration can indicate a thrips infestation. Thrips larvae appear translucent yellowish and sometimes have a black ball of fluid attached to their tail end—that's their excrement.

OPPOSITE BOTTOM ROW: Adult thrips are small slender black insects that crawl slowly on the leaf surface. Here's an adult roaming the surface of a *Monstera deliciosa*.

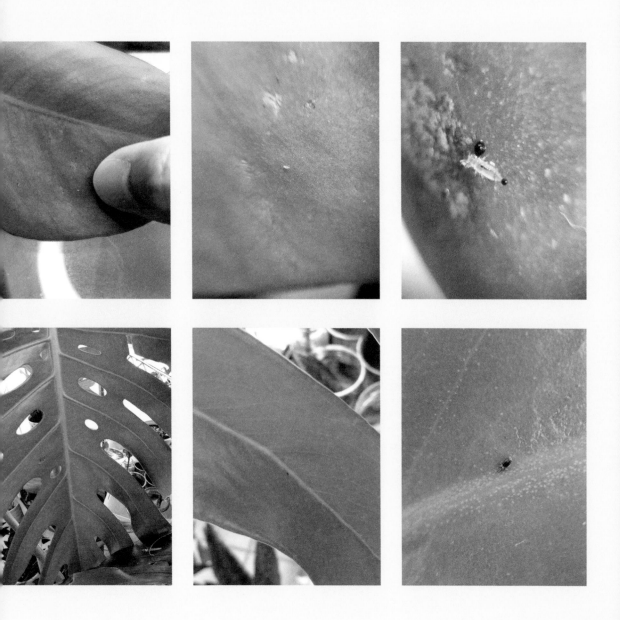

Acknowledgments

Aaron Apsley @apsley_watercolor

Begonia Flora @begonia_flora

Canadian Succulents, Molly Shannon @canadiansucculents

Centered By Plants @centeredbyplants

Crystal Star Nursery @crystalstarnursery

Dave's Air Plant Corner @davesairplantcorner

Dynasty Toronto @dynastyplantshop

Kim's Nature @kims_nature

Mike Rimland @costafarms

Justin W. Hancock @justinwhancock

Mason House Gardens, Jeff Mason @masonhousegardens

Jesse Goldfarb @teentinyterra

Melissa Maker @cleanmyspace @melissamaker

Tiffany Mah @plantmahmah

Melissa Lo @houseplant.oasis

Mulhall's Garden & Home @mulhalls

New York Botanical Garden @nybg

Tonkadale Greenhouse @tonkadale

Valleyview Gardens, Larry Varlese @valleyviewgardens

Vandermeer Nursery & Garden Centre @vandermeernursery

Chau Wa Chong & Nen Wa Chu

Woodhill Garden Centre @woodhillgardencentre

Special thanks to:

Soumeya B. Roberts

I always appreciate the work you've done for me, your guidance and encouragement. Thank you for representing and believing in me!

Eric Himmel

Thank you for bringing forth the idea for *The New Plant Collector* and for working with me along the way.

Cathleen McAllister

It was such a pleasure to work with you! Thank you for bringing my ideas to life.

Sebit Min

I was so excited that you would be designing my book again—really love how it all came together!

Mick Mulhall + Mulhall's team

Thanks for all your support and for bringing me into the Omaha plant community.

Jacqueline Chan

Your love and encouragement is what got me through the challenges in writing this book. Love you lots, my dear!

—Darryl Cheng

Image Credits

Illustrations by Cathleen McAllister: pp. 85, 94, 125, 133, 149, 161, 173

All photographs copyright © 2024 Darryl Cheng, except the following:

Kay Abadam @inrootedlove: pp. 151, 152, 153 (top right)

Brian Atchue @hanginghouseplants @brianthurium: pp. 59, 60 (right)

Alison Clements and Wade Kimmon @plantingpnw: pp. 61, 222

Jan Gettmann @ sydneyplantguy: pp. 179, 183 (top left)

Eric Himmel: pp. 12, 200 (left)

Roos Kocken @plantwithroos: pp. 74 (above; left), 86 (above, right), 166

Benson Kua: pp. 73 (right), 85 (left), 190 (above)

Jon Lane @daydreambeleafers: p. 195

Natasha Ling-LeBlanc @plantasha.to: pp. 136, 199

Tim Lung @urbangreenroomtropicals: p. 60 (left)

Tanya Martinovic @zenthegarden: pp. 4–5, 92

Dustin Miller @here_butnot: pp. 169 (top right; right), 185 (bottom right)

Vanessa Nghiem @bahnaesa: back cover p. (bottom left), 91

Melissa Oxendine @plantsbymelissa: pp. 135, 168 (above right)

Jainey Paz @paz_plantlife: pp. 131, 134

Beverly Phillips @turquoise.pot. alert: p. 97 (top left; above)

PT Prisma Tekno Kultura @exotropical.id: pp. 201 (left; top right), 202 (bottom right)

Molly Shannon @canadiansucculents: p. 80

Muhammad Ikhwan Shobari A.P.D., @gope.green: p. 67 (top left; bottom left)

Cyril Sontillano @cyrilcybernated: pp. 111, 184 (right)

Andrew Szeto @thepupandbud: p. 155 (bottom center)

Wing Hong Tse @kims_nature: p. 114 (top left)

Grace Vergara @wildleaf. toronto: p. 86 (above right)

Genna Weber @gennasplants: back cover (bottom right), pp. 126 (top left and right), 146 (above), 148, 153 (top left), 168 (above; bottom right), 185 (top left)

Elliot Yao @plantyiu: pp. 187, 190 (right)

Vivian Yu @fat_plants_only: pp. 122 (top; bottom), 128 (top; bottom)

Index

Editor: Eric Himmel
Designer: Sebit Min
Managing Editors: Glenn Ramirez
and Lisa Silverman
Production Manager:
Anet Sirna-Bruder

Library of Congress Control Number:
2023940296

ISBN: 978-1-4197-6150-8
eISBN: 978-1-64700-653-2

Printed and bound in China
10 9 8 7 6 5 4 3 2 1

Abrams Image books are available
at special discounts when purchased in quantity for premiums and
promotions as well as fundraising
or educational use. Special editions
can also be created to specification.
For details, contact specialsales@
abramsbooks.com or the address
below.

ABRAMS The Art of Books
195 Broadway, New York, NY 10007
abramsbooks.com